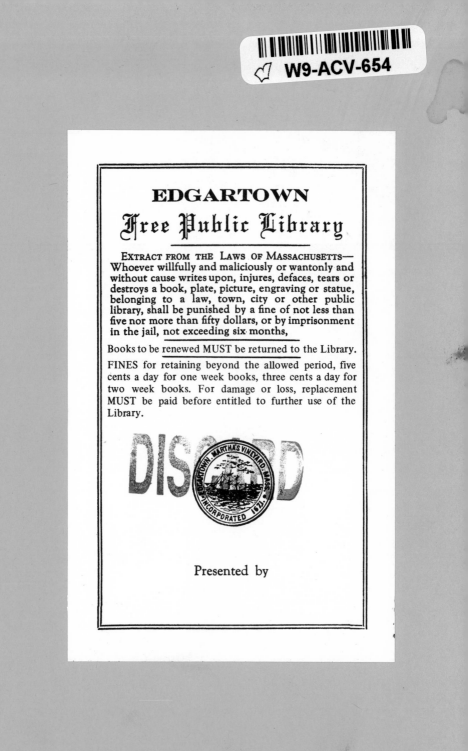

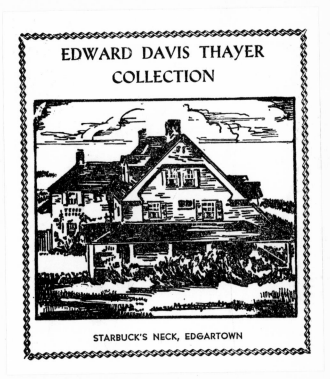

Marxism:
For and Against

Books by Robert L. Heilbroner

Robert L. Heilbroner

Marxism:
For and Against

W · W · NORTON & COMPANY

NEW YORK · LONDON

Published simultaneously in Canada by George J. McLeod Limited, Toronto.
Printed in the United States of America.

First Edition

Library of Congress Cataloging in Publication Data
Heilbroner, Robert L
  Marxism, for and against.
  Includes index.
  1. Marxian economics.   2. Dialectical materialism.
3. Socialism.   I. Title.
HB97.5.H37   1980   335.4   79–20385
ISBN 0–393–01307–3

for my colleagues and students

Contents

Acknowledgments

I HAVE DEDICATED this book to my colleagues and students because it has evolved from a long dialogue with them—a dialogue that has gradually brought me to the views set forth in these pages. Without saddling either colleagues or students with any responsibility for these views, I must make known my appreciation for the encouragement and criticism I have received from them. I could not have written the book without their help.

As so often in the past, I must place the name of Adolph Lowe at the head of my list of debts. There are few people who embody the attitude of *for and against* that I have taken as my own stance toward Marxism, but Adolph Lowe is one of these. I have relied heavily not only on his learning, but on his moral and aesthetic judgment.

Second, I am happy to write the name of Ronald Blackwell, who placed the extraordinary depth and breadth of his scholarship in Marx at my disposal, and who patiently read many drafts of the manuscript, and guided me away from misstatements and misunderstandings. Although Blackwell is as yet a graduate student and I am long a professor, in this undertaking the roles were more often than not reserved, to my great benefit.

Third, I wish to thank Stanley Burnshaw for a painstaking reading of the text, freeing it from many ambiguities and obscurities, and lending it an informed, skeptical, and insightful understanding.

I shall mention only in passing the names of other colleagues and students who have helped me with their advice: John Ernst, David Gordon, Kenneth Gordon, Virginia Held, and Anwar Shaikh. Lest I should inadvertently expose them to political risk, I omit with regret the names of two Iranian students who helped me greatly. Once again Lillian Salzman has brought forth a shining manuscript from a dreadful mess. And in the place of honor traditionally reserved for the end, I salute Shirley Heilbroner, who sustained me and endured my work, and thereby made the whole endeavor possible.

ROBERT L. HEILBRONER

New York City, May 1979

ONE

Introduction

MARXISM IS AN unsettling presence in the modern world, the source of the most passionate hopes and fears, the most contradictory visions. But I do not want to begin a study of the subject by plunging directly into these troubled waters. Instead, let me pose a question that may stir my reader's interest rather than his or emotions: Why is it that the work of Marx, from which Marxism springs, exerts such fascination after more than a century? Or as the matter is often put: why should we still turn to Marx for insight into contemporary affairs, when the world has changed almost out of recognition from the time in which he wrote?

I think it is possible to answer these questions in a way that sheds light on the continued survival of Marxism in the face of a hundred debunkings and "disproofs." It is that Marx had the good fortune, combined, of course, with the necessary genius, to create a method of inquiry that imposed his stamp indelibly on the world. We turn to Marx, therefore, not because he is infallible, but because he is inescapable. Everyone who wishes to pursue the kind of investigation that Marx opened up, finds Marx there ahead of him, and must thereafter agree with or confute, expand or discard, explain or explain away the ideas that are his legacy.

This kind of persisting influence is not, of course, unique to Marx. Perhaps the most striking example is that of Plato whose presence within philosophy is also inescapable. Before Plato, philosophers contented themselves with statements about the nature of things or about human understanding, but their dicta—however arresting and brilliant—lacked the power of structured argument. It was Plato's contribution to formulate a mode of philosophical discourse that emphasized reason, the meaning of words, and the crucial relationship between the knower and the known. In a sense, Plato thereby "invented" the task of systematic philosophy itself, which is why his influence is felt today even among philosophers who come to conclusions that are the opposite of his.

A similar persisting contemporaneity belongs to Freud. As with philosophy before Plato, there were certainly observers of the unconscious before Freud. But their insights and aperçus lacked force or conviction because they were not articulated as part of a whole, or arrived at by a specified method. Freud's discovery of the unconscious as an integral part of mental life irreversibly changed the conception of the human psyche. Thus, whether or not present-day observers subscribe to Freud's particular theories or use his specific techniques, his presence, like Plato's, is insistently at hand in the very task of psychoanalytic investigation itself.

Marx's importance derives from precisely such an achievement. His contribution, in some ways paralleling those of Plato and Freud, was the discovery of an unsuspected level of reality beneath the surface of history, above all beneath the history of the period that we call "capitalism." What Marx invented—again paralleling Plato and Freud—was a mode of inquiry to reach that buried reality, a mode we may call *socioanalysis*. Finally, as was the case with Plato, and as would again be the case with Freud, Marx's combination of insight and method permanently altered the manner in which reality would thereafter be perceived.[1]

That is why, despite the changes that time has brought, Marx's *Capital* is still germane and relevant in a way that Adam Smith's *Wealth of Nations*, for all its marvelous discernment, is not. The difference is not merely that Marx's work is more modern than Smith's because of its emphasis on technology and crises and social tensions. The deeper reason is that *Capital* undertakes a task quite without precedent in Smith or anyone else, a task indicated by its subtitle: *A Critique of Political Economy*. This critique begins with the misperceptions the system imposes on those who have not learned to penetrate its façade, and who therefore remain at the level of its surface manifestations. Marx's first purpose is to show how the everyday concepts by which we seek to elucidate society—concepts such as "labor" or "capital"—are, in fact, deceiving outward appearances that we must learn to pierce, if we are to understand the actual processes of social existence. We

[1]Since first arriving at this explanation for Marx's "inescapable" influence, I have learned that the French Marxist philosopher Louis Althusser has presented a similar explanation for Marx's unique place, claiming that Marx did for history what Thales did for mathematics, Galileo for physics, and Freud for psychology. See Althusser, *Lenin and Philosophy* (New York: Monthly Review Press, 1971), p. 15.

read *Capital*, therefore, not merely to discover how capitalism works, for Marx's explanation, though brilliant, is certainly imperfect, but to learn what capitalism *is*, the hitherto unposed question that Marx answers in a profound and unforgettable way.[2]

All these matters must, of course, be taken up and explained as we go along. But I hope that this first view of Marx as the founder of a method of socioanalysis gives us some idea as to why he remains immediate and indispensable, although many details of his explanation have been proved wrong. Not everyone dares to pierce the façade of society, just as not everyone is willing to venture into the rarified world of philosophical thought or the disconcerting realm of unconscious forces. But for those who want to explore the hidden dynamics of the life of society, Marx is the magisterial figure from whom we must all learn if we are to carry on the task of critical inquiry that he began.

The legacy of Marx is not, however, just a new vantage point from which to explore society. It also encompasses a body of work that has sprung into exis-

---

[2]The first readers of *The Wealth of Nations* may have felt a similar deep impact, when Smith explained to them not only how the economic system functioned, but that an Invisible Hand bestowed order and structure where the uninstructed eye saw only disorder and happenstance. Smith's insight was certainly an extraordinary piece of analysis that has permanently affected our understanding. But it was not quite socioanalysis, because Smith did not perceive the particular distortions of perception imposed by capitalist society. He saw mechanisms, but not ideologies, in society; and therefore the idea of a self-conscious "critique" of the efforts to understand society did not occur to him. As a result, his comprehension of the mechanisms, including the Invisible Hand, was circumscribed by assumptions of which he was not himself aware. See R. L. Heilbroner, "The Paradox of Progress," *Essays on Adam Smith* (New York: Oxford University Press, 1976), pp. 524f.

tence to support, supplement, and in some cases to supersede Marx's own writing—a body of work that, taken in its entirety, constitutes much of the pervasive "presence" of Marxism.

As with Marx himself, I want to take a preliminary measure of this larger presence. This brings us immediately to the problem of how to define Marxism itself. From the beginning, the work of Marx's followers has been characterized by bitter divisions and conflicting interpretations of Marx's work. But in recent years the divisions have become so pronounced and the interpretations so diverse that it is genuinely difficult to find the elements that unify the whole. Today there are Marxists who defend Marx's work as it stands and Marxists who would change nearly all of it; Marxists who feel that capitalism works essentially as Marx said it did, and Marxists who feel that the analysis of *Capital* no longer applies; Marxists who wish to reach out to religion and psychoanalysis and Marxists who feel that these are mere bourgeois diversions; Marxists who proudly call themselves orthodox and others who feel that Marxism has degenerated into ideology and is itself the chief obstacle to the attainment of a humane socialism. Indeed, the confusion of voices is so great that Eugene Kamenka, a lifelong scholar of Marxism, has declared that "the only serious way to analyze Marxist or socialist thinking may well be to give up the notion that there is a coherent doctrine called Marxism. . . ."[3]

[3]Quoted in Daniel Bell, "The Once and Future Marx," *American Journal of Sociology*, July 1977, p. 196.

Nevertheless, I believe there *is* a recognizable identity to Marxist thought—or, more accurately, to the thought inspired by Marx's writings to which we give the portmanteau description of "Marxism." This identity comes from a common set of premises that can be discovered in all such writing, no matter how strict or iconoclastic the viewpoints to which the writer subscribes or how inconsistent such views may be with one another. To put it differently, I believe that a set of premises exists that *defines* Marxist thought, so that any analysis that contains these premises can be properly classified as "Marxist" even if the writer does not identify it as such himself. Since these common premises will organize our own discussion, I should like to touch on them very briefly, to place in the reader's hand the Ariadne's thread that will guide us through the chapters ahead.

The first of these identifying elements is a *dialectical approach to knowledge itself.* Dialectics is a mystifying word, all too often used to sprinkle a kind of holy water over a subject or to vouch for the writer's true faith. But I believe there is a comprehensible core to dialectics which is uniformly, although often only tacitly, present in work that springs from Marx. This dialectical core is principally revealed in a view that considers the innermost nature of things to be dynamic and conflictual rather than inert and static; a view, therefore, that searches within things for their "contradictory" attributes.

Needless to say, this idea will be discussed more carefully. But meanwhile let us turn to a second element that also gives unity and identity to Marxist thought. This is its *materialist approach to history*. As with dialectics, "materialism" is by no means simple to define, nor without its serious problems. I think it can be described with reasonable accuracy as a perspective that highlights the central role played in history by the productive activities of mankind, and that therefore locates a principal motive for historical change in the struggle among social classes over their respective shares in the fruits of production. Clearly this conflictual view of history bears an affinity to the conflictual perspective of a dialectic philosophy.

A third common element is *a general view of capitalism that starts from Marx's socioanalysis.* As we have said, this does not lead every investigator to conclusions about the outcome of the system that are in accord with those of Marx. But without exception it means that writers in Marx's tradition accept and begin from, even if they modify, an understanding of what capitalism "is" that derives from Marx's original insight. In turn, this insight is recognizable as the application of the dialectical view of history to the present.

Last and not least is *a commitment to socialism,* defined in one form or another. There is another way of describing this final and very important common denominator of thought. It is to identify, as a necessary premise of Marxist writing, a belief in the "unity of theory and practice," a belief that the application of Marx's methods of analysis will not only shed light on the past but will serve as a guide to the creation of a socialist future, a future consciously made by mankind

21

for its own fulfillment. That belief, as we shall see, has encountered great difficulties. But the commitment to socialism as a desirable goal for humankind—and further, a goal to which Marxism will provide a useful guide—remains an integral element uniting all Marxist views.

One can no doubt argue against any attempt to organize so vast a structure as Marxist thought. This is especially the case because the work of Marx himself has a tighter focus than this larger panorama would suggest. Marx devoted his entire energy to the investigation of the social formation called capitalism, pressing into service for this end a dialectical method and a materialist interpretation of history, but never self-consciously attempting to construct a full-blown philosophy or a complete theory of history apart from his immense, but still circumscribed, purpose. The work of Marx's followers, however, spreads wider than that of Marx; and it is this larger scope of the Marxian legacy with which this book is concerned, as well as with Marx's work itself.

From the point of view of this larger scope, I think the framework outlined above serves a useful purpose. It makes it possible to separate, with a fair degree of accuracy, work that deserves to be called Marxist from work that does not, and thereby offers some bounds to our subject. In addition, the framework of premises offers another clue to the resilience and vitality of Marxism. For it allows us to see Marxism as embodying the promise of a grand synthesis of human understanding—a synthesis that begins with a basic philosophic perspective, goes on to apply this perspective to the interpretation of history, moves thereafter to an analysis of the present as the working-out of historical forces in the existing social order, and culminates in an orientation to the future that continues the line of analysis in an unbroken trajectory of action. Only a very few Marxists have tried to articulate or formulate this immense project. But the possibility lurks in the background of Marxist thought as a consequence of the connectedness of its central ideas. Marxism can thus be viewed as an effort to infuse a hitherto lacking coherence and meaning into social existence, not least into that aspect of existence that concerns our personal engagement with the society surrounding us.

To what extent Marxism succeeds in this lofty ambition is another matter, to which we will pay considerable heed. But in a world troubled by the fragmentation of knowledge and the meaninglessness of life, some part of the "presence" that Marxism obtrudes upon the world is surely the consequence of its unifying tendencies and its teleological thrust.

There remains a second problem to be discussed before we settle down to a systematic consideration of the ideas of Marxism. This is the relation of Marxism as a body of thought emanating from the work of Marx (and, of course, including that work itself), and the political realities of the Soviet Union, China, Cuba, and other self-styled "Marxist" states. The problem, I need hardly explain, is that all these states declare their indebtedness to Marx and their dedication to the principles of Marxism, while evidencing in their institutions and ideologies, attitudes that are abhorrent to most Westerners, including the great majority of Western Marxists.

The study of Marxism is thus clouded over and emotionally charged by the insistent question of the relation between—and the responsibility of—Marxism as an intellectual achievement and Marxism as a political fact. This is a problem for which there is some analogy in the question of the relation between capitalism and the activities of the United States, say, in Vietnam; or between Christianity and the Inquisition. Opponents of capitalism and Christianity have always asserted that such connections are direct and inseparable; defenders have asserted that they are only indirect and accidental. So it is with the problem of Marxism and its institutional realization. That there is *some* relation, *some* responsibility, is arguable. The difficulty lies in defining the nature of the linkage.

I shall have more to say about this matter in our final chapter. I raise the issue now only to recognize a raw question that would interfere with our work if it were not given explicit notice. But, for the moment, without asking of my readers an impossible degree of open-mindedness, I urge that we let the question remain in the background, keeping it in sight without allowing it to monopolize our attention. For I think it is important that we approach the subject of Marxism in a manner that is not only critical and questioning, but affirmative and sympathetic. This is because I believe, along with Jean-Paul Sartre, that Marxism is the "necessary" philosophy of our time, by which I mean that it affords a crucial insight into the historical and social predicaments of our lives. That does not imply that Marxism gives us an omniscient interpretation of our historical plight, any more than Plato answers all the questions of being or knowledge, or Freud explains all the processes of the unconscious. To be enlightened is not to be all-knowing. It is only to see a little further or to understand a little more deeply. That indeed is what the work of Marx and his followers allows us to do.

This raises a last problem surrounding the general subject of Marxism—a problem that is tempting to ignore or downplay because of the emotional conflicts it arouses: the nature of Marxism as a revolutionary doctrine. Heretofore we have been considering Marxism largely in terms of its intellectual content. But the unsettling presence of Marxism, the source of the contradictory visions for which it is responsible, does not lie in this content, important though it may be. As both its friends and foes assert, the *raison d' être* of Marxism lies in its commitment to a political goal, namely the overthrow (although not necessarily by violence) of the capitalist order and its replacement by a socialist, eventually, a communist one.

The revolutionary core of Marxism has obvious ramifications with the previous question of Marxism as a political reality. But the problem it poses is not quite the same. The revolutionary impetus and inspiration of Marxism would affect our inquiry even if the Russian Revolution had never taken a Stalinist turn, or if the

Soviet Union tomorrow were to become wholly democratic. For the act of revolution, with the alterations it portends for our life chances—and prior to the act, the images, the hopes, the fantasies of revolution—exerts an immense magnetism on, or imparts a powerful repulsion to, all observers for reasons that have little or nothing to do with Marxism as a body of reasoned inquiry or with the pathological possibilities of Marxism as a political movement. The self-declared objective of Marxism as a force for revolutionary change, as a rallying ground for the oppressed of the earth, polarizes virtually everyone with whom it comes into contact— *for* or *against*.

This brings me to my own stance, announced in the title of this book: for *and* against. This is a stance that will be rejected as inconsistent—worse, as suspicious, even intolerable—by readers drawn to one or another of the great poles of the revolutionary magnet. I shall not try to defend it at this point. I ask only that those who scrutinize my words for their subversive message from the perspective of one pole recognize that these self-same words will be regarded with an identical distrust by those who read them from the other pole. While that is no guarantee of their worth, it will at least advise my readers that I think another attitude toward Marxism is possible, beyond that of total embrace or rejection.

TWO

The Dialectical Approach to Philosophy

THERE is a great temptation to avoid the thorny subject of dialectics and to move immediately to the problem of capitalism with which Marxism is most immediately and deeply concerned. But I think this would be a mistake. All views of the world express philosophical premises, tacitly if not explicitly, and it is often at this half-exposed level that their ultimate strengths or their weaknesses are located. This is particularly the case with Marxism which is self-consciously built on a philosophic foundation whose concepts and vocabulary run through its writings like a colored thread.

Thus the most important reason to begin a study of Marxism with an examination of dialectics is simply to become familiar with a vocabulary that is inseparable from Marxist thought—a task all the more necessary because the vocabulary of dialectics is not generally familiar, even to most contemporary philosophers. Looking through the journals of modern philosophy, especially in the United States and England, one rarely comes across the word *dialectic*, much less a discussion of "dialectical" problems. Indeed, with the exception of a few European or Marxist philosophers, well out of the mainstream, the entire approach is no longer taken seriously.

Another reason to start with dialectics, therefore, is to interpret it to those who believe that its vocabulary is mere obfuscation and pointless complexity. Obviously I do not hold this to be true. As I shall try to make clear, I think there are problems for which we require the special vocabulary and distinct perspective that are called "dialectical"—problems that remain invisible or recalcitrant before the gaze and techniques of more conventional philosophic approaches.

At the same time, I also wish to make clear the limitations, as well as the reach, of a dialectical approach. If dialectics is to be explained to beginners, and legitimated to philosophers, it must be rescued from those who use its terminology as an evidence of piety, or who flash its words as a badge of authority. Thus there is an *against* as well as a *for* in my initial undertaking, both aspects of which will, I trust, become clear as we proceed.

(1)

It would be useful if I could now start straight off with an exposition of dialectics. But I cannot. The reason is that there is no single established meaning for dialectics, and still less so for the dialectics incorporated within Marxism. I am forced to begin, therefore, with an attempt to define our subject by the process of successive approximations, slowly narrowing the circle of definitions until we have established what Marxian dialectics is not, as well as what it is.

The word *dialectics* comes from the Greek term for dialogue, and a residue of give-and-take, of relentless questioning, continues to inform the concept. At the core of all varieties of dialectics, we find a continuation of that incessant querying, that active engagement with the resistant stuff of knowledge, so unforgettably portrayed by Plato in the person and style of Socrates, the great exponent of the dialectical method in classical philosophy.[1]

For Marxism, the legacy of this Greek sense of a dialectical questioning process resides in an "activist" attitude toward knowledge itself. A Marxian approach to philosophy stresses the *production,* rather than the passive receipt of knowledge—the involvement of the act of inquiry in shaping, as well as in discovering, knowledge. Because Marxian dialectics maintains that knowledge is not bestowed but won, it maintains that there is a deep, and indeed indissoluble, bond between what the Greeks called *praxis* or action, and *theoria* or thought—between "doing" and "thinking."[2] Thus, the unity of theory and practice that we have already noted in passing as an integral element of the Marxist commitment to socialism finds its roots in the dialectical insistence that "philosophizing" can only be vindicated and validated by some kind of activity; that reality is not merely what "is," but what we make it.

This activist orientation, as we shall see in our next

[1]Dialectics in Plato refers mainly to a mode of argumentation that includes refuting an opponent by drawing unacceptable conclusions from his premises. Plato extolls this "dialectic" and denigrates "eristic"—what we would call sophistry. See, for example, *The Republic,* Book VII.

[2]Cf. Richard Bernstein, *Praxis and Action* (Philadelphia: University of Pennsylvania Press, 1971), pp. ix, x.

chapter, is the source of both strength and difficulty for Marxism. But first we must search for an understanding of the ways in which a dialectical vision of things differs from a nondialectical one. Here we must pay heed to another Greek root of dialectical thought, exemplified by Heraclitus, the famous originator of the problem of stepping twice into the "same" river. From this point of view we derive a second basic idea of dialectics, as profoundly important as it is elusive. This is that the ultimate and irreducible nature of all reality is motion, not rest, and that to depict things as static or changeless is to disregard or violate the essence of their being.

We shall shortly see that this concept leads to important conclusions. But I think it useful to halt for a moment at this early stage of our inquiry. For in the idea of immanent change as the fundamental nature of reality, we can already discover both an advantage for dialectics—a perception not available from a nondialectical standpoint—and a limitation.

The advantage is immediately obvious. A Heraclitean depiction of the universe, with its emphasis on the changefulness of all things, strikes the Western mind as an intuitively right approach to reality, in tune with our temperament, our understanding of things. The difficulty comes when we try to subject this intuitively right grasp of things to systematic examination. Then we find that the very characteristic of changefulness that commends a dialectical viewpoint to our imaginations renders it awkward for our cognitive faculties. It is difficult to "think" about change, even if it is natural to imagine it. Heraclitus's river is much more easily discussed in its infinite instants of motionlessness than in its single trajectory of movement. Therefore when we turn to philosophic discussion we find ourselves naturally inclining toward a view of the universe that stops its processes, like so many frames of a motion picture, in order to allow us to examine things as if they were actually suspended motionless in space and time.

Thus, if there is a natural resonance between the dialectical "vision" of existence and our psychological processes, there is a difficulty in subjecting this vision to intellectual inspection. In this disjunction between the imaginative and the ratiocinative properties of our minds lies an important insight, I believe, into the problem of dialectics. Already it makes clear that a dialectical approach offers an entree into the possible nature of things that is blocked to view from a non-dialectical perspective; but it also makes clear that the vision we gain cannot easily be turned to use by the procedures of normal inquiry.

(2)

The conception of the universe as inherently changeful readies us for the next step in the definition of Marxian dialectics. We must now move from Greek origins to the work of Hegel, without question the philosopher who exercised the greatest influence over Marx himself and over the subsequent development of a Marxian dialectics.

Hegel's thought is profound and forbidding, an elaboration on an immense scale of the ideas of Being and Becoming, which manifest themselves through all of nature and history in a vast process of self-transcendence called the dialectic. Marx was greatly influenced by the grandeur and internal dynamics of Hegel's scheme, although not by the primacy that it accorded to *logos*, or pure thought. Describing Hegel as "that mighty thinker," Marx emphasized that his own version of the dialectical method rested on the world of material things, not on that of thought.[3]

In our next chapter we will examine the idea of a dialectic of materialism. But if Marx turned Hegel upside down, he also retained an idea central to the Hegelian notion of dialectics. This was a conception of change as consisting not in mere movement or displacement, enlargement or diminution, but in *qualitative alteration*. In turn this qualitative alteration arose not from the impingement of "forces" on inert things—that would still ultimately rest on a static conception of reality—but from a universal changefulness located "within" things that Hegel called *contradiction*.

Because the idea of contradiction will occupy us for much of this chapter, and because the word presents great difficulties for conventional philosophers and equally great temptations for self-serving Marxist use, we must stop to examine the term. In ordinary speech contradiction has a clear meaning: we cannot properly make two assertions with regard to something, if one assertion denies the other. Thus, we cannot say that a stone exists and that it does not exist, referring to the same stone at the same instant. Or rather, if we do make such an assertion, we forfeit any possibility of carrying

---

[3]*Capital*, I, Postface to 2nd edition. [All citations from *Capital*, Volume I, refer to the Vintage Books edition, edited by Ben Fowkes, 1977. References to volumes II and III concern the International Publishers edition, 1967.] For a discussion of Hegel's influence on Marx, see Iring Fetscher, *Marx and Marxism* (New York: Herder and Herder, 1971), or for a more controversial view, Lucio Colletti, *From Rousseau to Lenin* (New York: Monthly Review Press, 1972).

on what we call a "reasoned" discussion, for one could then assert any number of incompatible and inconsistent things. Thus to declare the illegitimacy of contradictions is simply to lay down one rule for mutual comprehension and discourse.

This kind of *logical contradiction* is not, however, the meaning of contradiction that applies to dialectics. In dialectics, the word does not refer to the simultaneous assertion and denial of the existence of static things; instead, it refers to the nature of those conflicting elemental processes that are believed to constitute the essence of reality itself. As a first rough description of what such a "contradiction" implies, we can resort to another famous Hegelian phrase—"the unity of opposites." Contradictions therefore refer to the idea that all of reality is changeful because it consists, in its very innermost being, of the unstable coexistence and successive resolution of incompatible forces. Thus the fundamental concept of Being itself implies Nonbeing; and from this joining of opposites there issues forth its resolution, Becoming—which also contains a similar contradiction and resolution.

I shall deliberately leave this description vague and unexplored for the moment, because it is an important part of my argument that we understand at an intuitive level what such a conception of "contradiction" means. Later we shall examine it further. Meanwhile, however, we can see that an affinity exists between this general dialectical vision and the tendencies that Marxism will discover in history—an affinity between the contradiction-laden idea of change as Hegel sees it, and the idea of the disruptive, yet creative, unfolding central to the Marxist analysis of history. Thus, even though Marxism is not a "philosophy," it is powerfully affected by its philosophic premises; and its dialectic vantage point conditions, even if it does not fully determine, its social perspective.

(3)

The idea of contradiction is the open-sesame of a dialectical philosophy, bringing into high relief problems that are indistinct or simply invisible from another point of view. As we shall see, the notion of contradiction gives us insights with respect to Being and Becoming in society—that is, insights into history. But there is also an illumination provided by the idea of contradiction at a simpler level: it enables us to perceive the complex, relational nature of ideas or entities that appear to the undialectical eye as simple or self-contained.

Hegel gives us a famous example of this elucidatory power in his discussion of the terms Master and Servant. The very concept of Master, he shows, implies the opposite of such a concept in the Servant, one who is mastered. Without the idea of one, we cannot form the idea of the other, although each idea "by itself" is the contradiction (the "negation," in Hegel's terminology) of the other.[4] Note that this use of contradiction does not assert that a Master "is" and "is not," which would involve us in the same absurdity as making that assertion about a stone. Rather, the point is that a Master is a being who can only be *defined* or *described* by using a concept that is its meaningful opposite or negation. Without Servants there are no Masters, and vice versa.

What emerges from this dialectical perspective is a

---

[4]*The Phenomenology of the Spirit* (from *The Philosophy of Hegel*) ed. C.J. Friedrich (New York: Modern Library, 1934), pp. 399f.

comprehension of existence that is of necessity more complex and ambiguous than that which emerges from a nondialectical approach to things. In turn, from this view in which objects are understood to exist in a mutually interacting "relational" context, Hegel constructs an entire theory of knowledge. It would, however, take us away from our main purpose to pursue that matter further. It is enough to note that the idea of contradiction provides the philosophic underpinning for the socioanalysis that Marxism will perform on the social world. For the kind of mutually determined relationship portrayed by Hegel in the example of Master and Servant will be enlarged and deepened by Marx in his examination of the ideas of Capital and Labor, where he will also discover internal contradictions similar to those identified by Hegel, but of much more striking political and historical import. This is a matter that we will look into again in Chapter IV.[5]

[5]For an illuminating discussion of Hegelian dialectics, see J.N. Findlay, "The Contemporary Relevance of Hegel" in *Hegel, a Collection of Critical Essays*, ed. Alasdair MacIntyre (New York: Doubleday, 1972). Findlay makes clear that the process of relating an idea and its contradictory opposite often involves our moving to a *higher level of abstraction*, in which the contradictories unite to create a new synthesis—from which, in turn, still larger complexities can be constructed. I have omitted this dimension of Hegelian thought as unnecessary for our present discussion. I should add that the contradiction e.g. of Master and Servant is by no means confined to their static definitions, but includes their conflictual interactions, which change the nature of both Master and Servant. This is an approach that we will pursue in our next section.

Finally, I should like to call attention to an exploration of the relational aspects of the dialectical view expounded by Richard Norman in "On Dialectic," *Radical Philosophy*, no. 14, Summer 1976. Norman suggests that dialectics can be seen as an effort to resolve the traditional impasse of views that stress matter over mind (materialism) and vice versa (idealism). Dialectics, according to Norman, seeks to resolve this unsatisfactory dualism by beginning with the concept of the *relationship* between mind and matter, a relationship that unites the two in the act of knowing, according the distinctive attributes to each, and reducing neither element to the other. From this relational viewpoint, Norman then examines the ideas of Universals and Particulars and other such famous antinomies, showing how they can be comprehended once we accept the idea of a conceptual contradiction as described above.

The relational complexity opened up by a dialectical examination of the world is still, however, a somewhat static application of the idea of contradiction. Closer to the Marxist usage of the term is its application to the flux and change characteristic of the social world. Here the category that corresponds in its relational complexity to a "concept" is a "process"—a sequence of events. The dialectic perspective allows us to call certain processes "contradictory" because they unfold in ways that are both integral to, and yet destructive of, the processes themselves.

An instance may make this clear. In Marx's own work, the concept of contradiction plays its most important role in analyzing the vast sociohistoric process of capitalism itself. For the idea of contradiction enables us to see that there is a certain dialectical "logic" to its historic tendencies, insofar as they emerge from and reflect the contradictory nature of the system. Perhaps the most famous of these self-negating tendencies is one that Marx discovers in the very core subprocess of the system, its accumulation of capital. It is in the nature of capitalism, as Marx describes it, that it must seek to expand, whether through business growth, or by the search for new ways to increase profits, or in financial operations to increase money capital. As we will later see, the struggle for expansion is an integral and inextricable element in the evolution of capitalism as a period of history. At the same time, however, this expansive aspect is constantly undermining the viability of the larger system. The necessity for business growth, for instance, creates the conditions of "anarchic" rivalry that threaten the system with crisis. The insatiable thirst for profits drives the business system into mechanization that augments profits in the short run, but that eliminates them in the long run. The financial manipulations induce, or magnify, economic disorder.

These complicated modes of capitalist operation will be studied when we examine Marx's socioanalysis of capitalism. What needs to be grasped now is that this analysis depicts the capitalist process as not merely beset by "problems," but beset by problems that are the underside of its "successes." In this way, a dialectical perspective, with its central idea of contradiction, reveals the connectedness of social events that might otherwise seem to be only accidentally conjoined.

It is well, however, that we conclude this exploration of the strengths of a dialectical perspective with two warnings. The first is that *the presence of conflicts within social processes does not in itself suffice to establish these conflicts as contradictions*. The social world, like the natural world, is full of opposing forces, most of which have no more "contradictory" significance than the chance encounter of two particles or the clash of two wills. Contradictions refer to those oppositions that are both necessary for, and yet destructive of, particular processes or entities. This is a distinction that we will meet again in considering the application of dialectics to history.

Thus the task of a dialectical inquiry is not to make sweeping statements about the omnipresence of contradictions, but to identify the particular contradictory tendencies, if any, within a given social process. This is not a matter to be taken for granted when beginning from a dialectical point of view. Two dialecticians, examining the same social panorama, may differ on the appropriate concepts or processes within which to seek contradictions, or having agreed on these, may disagree as to the nature of their contradictory elements. In a word, dialectics provides an angle of vision, a lens through which to view society, but it does not predetermine what will be discovered there. These strictures apply in particular to the use of a dialectical vocabulary by some Marxists to establish the very problem that ought to be demonstrated. To use the word contradiction loosely, applying it to conflicts that have not been shown to be both necessary for the maintenance and decisive for the destruction of a social process, is to waste the real strength of a dialectical philosophy by debasing it into mere rhetoric.

The second warning is that *a dialectical approach in itself sheds no light on the actual sequences of events through which contradictory tendencies work themselves out.* Even if a dialectical perspective enables one unfailingly to identify the forces of contradiction in any social situation, the perspective does not describe the sequential happenings by which the contradiction works its effects on the social system. For example, the insight that the emergence of large-scale organized enterprise is both an apotheosis of capitalism and an entering wedge of socialism does not describe the particular ways in which large-scale enterprise grows, or the specific manner in which it will affect the ongoing "metabolism" of capitalism, or the precise fashion in which its technology or organization may become the foundation for a planned economic system. Indeed, these are matters about which Marxists disagree as vigorously as non-Marxists.

Thus the dialectical perspective affords insight into

relationships, but not into causal sequences. It offers a heuristic—a diagnostic or revelatory—approach but no special technique to implement that approach. Problems that may remain hidden to a nondialectical view are opened for exploration, but the conclusions to which those explorations may lead are not themselves prescribed by the dialectical perspective itself.

For all its elucidating power, the central idea of contradiction remains a problem for many critics of a dialectical philosophy, and before moving on, I wish to explore this problem a little more deeply.

The difficulty arises, I believe, because many critics continue to interpret "contradiction" in its logical, Aristotelian sense in which the contradiction of A is not-A. This easily reduces dialectical usage to violations of sense and meaning, as Sir Karl Popper shows in *Conjectures and Refutations* and elsewhere. But that is not the meaning that contradiction holds as a relational view of the world. The *logical* contradiction (or "opposite" or "negation") of a Master is not a Slave, but a "not-Master," which may or may not be a slave. But the *relational* opposite of a Master is indeed a Slave, for it is only by reference to this second "excluded" term that the first is defined. Paul Diesing clearly describes this usage:

Two concepts are dialectically related when the elaboration of one draws attention to the other as an opposed concept that has been implicitly denied or excluded by the first; when one discovers that the opposite concept is required (presupposed) for the validity or applicability of the first; and when one finds that the real theoretical problem is that of the interrelationship between two concepts, and the real descriptive problem that of determining their interrelations in a particular case.

The same necessity to think in terms of relationships applies to the strictures of Popper and others regarding the "thesis, antithesis, synthesis" type of argument. Popper has no difficulty in showing that a given thesis does not produce an antithesis as its *logical* opposite. But a thesis may indeed produce an antithesis (or contradiction) when it is viewed *as a process to be understood from a relational vantage point,* and not simply as a statement to be asserted and denied. Parenthetically, neither Marx nor Hegel ever used the "thesis, antithesis, synthesis" formulation. We owe the phrase to Fichte.

The most vexing question for a Marxian view of dialectics, to be sure, has to do with the legitimacy of locating contradictions in nature itself. One can ascribe a dialectical—that is, immanently changeful and contradictory—aspect to all reality as a basic, unchallengeable assumption. Unfortunately, that reduces the idea of contradiction to a tautology, of heuristic but not operational usefulness. For if all of nature is contradictory by assumption, nothing is gained by pointing to the contradictory aspect of any particular element within it.

The problem, therefore, is to try to distinguish contradiction as a universal aspect of nature, and contradiction as an identificatory attribute of particular natural or social processes. Here I believe the way out lies in the conception of the "unities" within which contradictions are to be found. Unities are concepts introduced into reality by our minds. The universe itself

is simply a flux, with innumerable collisions and interactions that have no unitary character, except insofar as
we create such a character by the act of perception and
comprehension. For example, the blast and recoil of a
gun are "contradictions" only insofar as we relate the
motions of particles that we designate as "blast" to the
reaction of the mass that we call "recoil." Without the
intervention of our intelligence, blast and recoil are no
more bound together than any of the infinite simultaneously occurring events in the universe. We can, of
course, describe blast and recoil as "contradictions,"
but in so doing we are not shedding light on the processes of nature, but on the unifying tendencies of our
minds.

It is when we turn to the social world that unities
become of immediate importance. We can imagine the
universe as a swarm of particles, without its thereby
ceasing to be a universe, whereas we cannot so imagine society. Without social, political, intellectual,
economic, or other unities, the social world has no
meaning. Thus we are *forced* to seek unities within the
realm of social existence under an imperative different
from that by which we establish them in nature, and in
the process of creating different kinds of social unities,
we discover the contradictory elements they contain.
Dialectics thereby has a natural application to the social
world that it lacks in the physical one.

One final point. Hegel circumvents the question of
whether contradictions exist in nature because he assumes that thought and reality have a common ground in
a preexisting "logos." Therefore there exists in Hegel
an identity of thought and existence that permits the idea

of contradiction to penetrate all of reality without running into the difficulties we have mentioned. It is because Marx and his followers reject this idealist basis of Hegelian thought, that Marxist dialectics encounters the problem of how to relate dialectical thought and natural processes.[6]

(4)

The emphasis on exploration takes us now to a last definition of dialectics. We have heretofore emphasized the "activist" search for knowledge with its interdependence of theory and practice; the "vision" of an imminently changeful reality; and the idea of contradiction within the categories and processes of social existence. All these are meanings that dialectics carries for Marxism. Now we must add a final dimension of meaning having to do with the pursuit of truth, namely the *method* by which inquiry is carried out.

The distinctive contribution that dialectics makes to methodology consists of its approach to the problem of forming concepts. Marx himself gives us perhaps the most brilliant example of this method when he asks, in the *Grundrisse*, how we can form the ideas with which political economy will operate.

It seems to be correct [he writes] to begin with the real and the concrete, . . . thus to begin in economics, with e.g. the population which is the foundation and the subject of the entire social act of production.

However on closer examination this proves false. The

<hr />

[6]Paul Diesing, *Patterns of Discovery in the Social Sciences* (Chicago: Aldine, 1971), p. 212. For an interesting exchange, see Lucio Colletti, "Marxism and the Dialectic," *New Left Review*, Sept.-Oct. 1975 and Roy Edgley, "Dialectic: The Contradictions of Colletti," *Critique*, no. 7, Winter 1976–77. See also Sidney Hook, *From Hegel to Marx* (New York: Humanities Press, 1950), pp. 75–76.

population proves an abstraction if I leave out, for example, the classes of which it is composed. These classes in turn are an empty phrase if I am not familiar with the elements on which they rest, e.g. wage labor, capital, etc. These latter in turn presuppose exchange, division of labor, prices, etc. . . .

Thus if I were to begin with the population, this would turn out to be a chaotic conception of the whole. I would then . . . move analytically toward ever simpler concepts, from the imagined concrete towards ever thinner abstractions until I arrived at the simplest determinations. From there the journey would have to be retraced until I had finally arrived at the population again, but this time not as a chaotic conception of a whole, but as a rich totality of many determinations and relations.[7]

On the face of it, this procedure is clear enough, involving a regress from superficial surface appearances to their underlying elements, followed by a reconstruction of the original datum in a much fuller context. The difficulty arises when we seek the method to implement the methodology—the specific instructions, the algorithms, the handbook of instructions for realizing each step along the road toward abstraction or back to concreteness. For then we discover that crucially important decisions must be made at each stage—deciding which abstract elements to pursue, disentangling "decisive" connections from accidental ones, specifying the process of analysis or reconstitution, judging the final result for its usefulness. What criteria shall we use in deciding, for instance, whether the population should originally be analyzed as consisting

---

[7]*Grundrisse: Foundations of the Critique of Political Economy,* trans. Martin Nicolaus, (New York: Penguin Books, 1973), pp. 100–101 (hereafter cited as *Grundrisse*). I have slightly altered paragraphing and punctuation for the sake of clarity.

of two social classes, or three, or more? In turn, by which criteria will we judge the decomposition of, say, labor into its constituent "determinations" to be accurate or inaccurate, complete or partial? Such questions cannot be side-stepped if the result of the dialectical methodology is to be defensible against attacks from empirical or other points of departure.[8]

Thus, as before, a dialectical approach yields a rich harvest for the imagination, but a scanty one for exact analysis. As an example of the insight it can offer, we should take note of Marx's profound analysis of "the individual"—the analytic focus of so much non-Marxist social science—as "the ensemble of social relations."[9] What appears to be the concrete entity of *an individual* can easily be shown to be a "chaotic conception" unless we pierce the façade of the solitary being to its social roots, and then reconstitute the individual as a person embedded in, and expressing, the social forces of a particular society. At the same time, the procedures for moving from the naive conception of the individual to his or her social determination and back again are left unspecified, so that two dialectical methodologists may well arrive at two different "rich totalities" of the final result—one, for example, emphasizing the socioeconomic roots of gender differences, the other

[8]The most ambitious recent attempt to reduce the dialectical method to a concrete sequence of steps is by Ernest Mandel, *Late Capitalism* (New York: New Left Books, 1975), pp. 16–17, where the method is presented in six stages of regress and reconstitution. Unfortunately, the six steps are described in words that continually beg the question. For instance, the first step (abbreviated) is "Comprehensive appropriation of the empirical material . . . in all its historically relevant detail." But how do we know what is relevant? And is not the decision as to what is and what is not relevant decisive for the path of further analysis? Mandel (or Marx) provide no means of testing this critical step or subsequent steps, so that the use of the dialectical method is not subject to any internal discipline.

[9]Marx, *Theses on Feuerbach, VI;* cf. also *Grundrisse,* p. 265.

stressing the sociopsychological roots of the same phenomenon. From one point of view, a woman is quintessentially an exploited being who also has female characteristics; from another, a woman is quintessentially a female being who is also exploited.

To be sure, there is an unavoidable element of arbitrariness in all methods of pursuing empirical knowledge. At best we can minimize that arbitrariness by imposing certain rules on the procedures we are allowed to follow. One of these, for instance, is the rule of ordinary logic—a rule that applies equally to dialectical and nondialectical thought. As we have seen, dialectics asserts that contradictions exist, but not in a sense that would violate the precepts of straightforward logic which prevent us from saying Yes and No simultaneously.

Another rule is that of science, which demands that the methods we follow be defensible by certain established canons of procedure. Here, too, Marxian dialectics joins with other approaches to knowledge in insisting on the "scientific" nature of its own procedures, *but it differs from other approaches in the way it defines science.*

The dominant notion of science today refers to a method of obtaining information about the world, a method that can be roughly described as the formulation of refutable hypotheses. There is no doubt that *social* science falls well short of these ideal specifications, but that is not the matter that interests us here. For the idea of science broached by Marx does not lie in devising testable hypotheses, but in a differently conceived task, namely, piercing the screen of appearances to arrive at

47

the "scientific" truth of a concealed essence. "All science would be superfluous if the outward appearance and the essence of things directly coincided," Marx wrote.[10] This is different from the approach of the nondialectical social scientist who does not concern himself with essences at all, indeed, who does not recognize the word.

A dialectical view of social science therefore poses an interpretive task quite different from that of modern day "positivism."[11] The positivist scientist also penetrates surface phenomena to arrive at underlying truths in the forms of "laws" or patterns, but his task is one of peering through *random* disturbances to discover regularities (not essences) presumably concealed within

---

[10]*Capital*, III, p. 817. Marx speaks of social inquiry only. Whether there is a Marxist science of nature that differs from conventional bourgeois science is a matter that once agitated Marxists during the years of Stalin's influence, but that has now subsided almost entirely. The question is, of course, related to the relevance of dialectics to nature, a matter discussed on pages 41–43.

[11]The canons of positivist science are not easy to abbreviate into a footnote. The main tenets of *positivism*, as a philosophic stance, are (1) a concern with empirical matters and an indifference to "metaphysical" ones, and (2) an attempt to draw a strict line between "synthetic" statements which are related to testable, empirical propositions, and "analytic" statements which involve only questions of logic or grammar. (For a clear exposition, see Hollis and Nell, *Rational Economic Man*, [New York: Cambridge University Press, 1975], pp. 4–10). A positivist *science* builds on this philosophical foundation by limiting itself to empirical problems that can be stated in testable hypothetical form. This canon is by no means always observed, but it does at least represent the positivist credo. The main objective of positivist science is accordingly to discover "lawlike" regularities that enable us to make predictive statements. There is no difference recognized by positivism between the tenets of social and natural science.

Dialectics does not deny the importance or validity of the work of the empirical experimenter, but seeks to expand the conception of the scientist's work beyond the borders of a positivist approach. It would, I think, be bolder in claiming an "explanatory" purpose, and less confident in claiming a predictive one. This seeming paradox is the consequence of the dialectical concern with interpretation and with the continuous "engagement" of the would-be knower struggling with the elusive appearances and essences of what-is-to-be-known. This does not lead to such clear-cut predictive laws as does a positivist approach. As we shall see in Chapter IV, however, a Marxist perspective can yield powerful prognostications that derive from the discovery of contradictions.

nature. The dialectical observer, on the contrary, tries to find real essences (not mere regularities), such as contradictory relations, by penetrating the *systematic* distortions imposed upon us by society.

These distortions—religious, political, social, economic—affect our vision in ways of which we are mainly unaware. The primary task of the dialectically minded social scientist, accordingly, is to inform us as to the presence and nature of our systematic misperceptions, so that we can discern essences where we would otherwise be deceived by appearances. What is dialectical about this scientific task is, of course, derived from the view that stresses the relational, contradictory aspect of social knowledge—a view that differs markedly from the approach of non-Marxist social science, with its emphasis on "facts" rather than contexts.

This is a powerful conception of science, at least within the realm of the social universe to which it is properly applicable. Indeed, the entire contribution of Marxism to social thought rests ultimately on its effort to penetrate the veil of appearances to discover the hidden essences of things, the web of relations that is the "real" ground of reality and not the surface manifestations that are its façade. *The target of a dialectical methodology is therefore illusion or delusion, not simple ignorance.* Marx's direct use of the word "scientific" was aimed, more than anywhere, at what he called "vulgar" conceptions of society.

Nonetheless, something is lacking from this penetrative method. It is the same lack we have noted before, namely, a rule for separating valid procedures from invalid ones; a test, however difficult to achieve in fact, that would enable us to discard some dialectical results as false. The dialectical approach to methodology leaves us with no means of appraising its results other than by the tests of conventional science, or those of ordinary logic.

The consequence is that Marxism has an uneasy relation to present-day positivist science. It scoffs at the "blatant empiricism" that is the credo of most social science, which it bitingly describes as gathering and collating facts with no theoretical vision to give them meaning and coherence. This is true enough. Yet a Marxist diagnosis of social events is repeatedly forced to establish its own "scientific" nature by subjecting its conclusions to the only testing procedures that we know—namely, those of empirical, positivist-oriented methods.

An illustration may be useful here. Two of Marx's most striking pronouncements, both grounded in his dialectical analysis of the contradictions of capitalism, were the tendency of capital to agglomerate in ever larger masses, and the tendency of the population to be reduced to the status of dependent wage earners. Both have been amply demonstrated by history (and will be discussed later). The "vindication" of these insights, however, rests entirely on recourse to ordinary empirical methods of observation and testing. Take, now, the dialectical insight that the rise of massive enterprise also creates the structural framework for socialism. There has been neither confirmation nor disconfirmation of this contradiction. Until we have such a test, however, it would be difficult even for Marxists to call the insight "scientific," in the sense of penetrating to the essence of things, for we do not yet know if this *is* the essence of things. A dialectical methodology thereby poses a new and striking vision of the truth that we want science to reveal, but gives us no dialectical test of the results of its application.

(5)

It is time to review our discussion and to hazard a conclusion. To sum up very rapidly the work of our preceding pages, we have seen that dialectics can be described in several distinct, although related ways: as a stance toward the acquisition of knowledge; as a conception of existence that stresses its fundamental and irreducible element of changefulness; as a conception of social entities that reveals them to be a unity of "contradictory opposites"; and as a method of forming concepts as a "rich totality of many determinations," obtained by an interpretative rather than a purely empirical approach to scientific investigation.

It must be apparent that these different meanings of dialectics operate on different planes. Its conceptions of the changeful and contradictory character of the universe are assumptions about the nature of reality. Its active stance and its methodological procedures concern the mode of investigation required to investigate nature as conceived in a dialectical way. And beyond these definitions lies yet another formulation of dialectics, largely confined to Marx's own writings—a formulation that seeks a distinctive method of presentation,

51

designed to reveal the appearances and the essences of its subject matter.[12]

In different ways, and with different applications, all these various approaches to, and meanings of, a dialectical philosophy seem to me to validate it as a mode of thought and to clarify its essential contributions to Marxism. Yet it is also clear that all these dialectical approaches bring with them a sharp sense of limitation. The dialectical view of existence as inherently changeful is intuitively attractive, but intellectually elusive. The identification of contradiction as an element of social reality yields new possibilities for social dissection, but it gives us no means of identifying what those contradictions are. A dialectical methodology has not found a way of reconciling its suggestive mode of forming concepts or of formulating the task of science with its continued reliance on nondialectical techniques to test the validity of its concepts or its science in use.

The question to be faced, then, is whether we can explain this curiously two-sided aspect of dialectics, at once so rich and so poor, so useful and so useless, so powerful and so impotent. I think there is an explanation, if we return to the contrast between the appeal to our imagination and the frustration of our intelligence

[12]This method is discussed by Marx in ''The Method of Political Economy,'' *Grundrisse*, pp. 100–108, and elucidated in Roman Rosdolsky's superb commentary, *The Making of Marx's Capital* (London: Pluto Press, 1977), pp. 25–55. Briefly, the method parallels the one previously discussed, in proceding from the abstract to the concrete and then to a larger reconstitution of the abstract. Marx himself uses the method both in structuring the sequence of argument in *Capital* as a whole, and in approaching various subtopics, such as the idea of surplus value and the length of the working day (I, Chapters 9 and 10), or the relation of capital accumulation to its primitive origins (I, Chapters 26–32). It may be that this usage of dialectics is the most significant (although not the only) meaning of the term for Marx himself, but in the larger canon of Marxist work it has become submerged in the other meanings discussed above.

that we noted at the outset. This initial dichotomy, which we now see repeated in many applications of dialectics, suggests that the contrast is not accidental, but reflects a deep-lying property of a way of apprehending reality, not quite the same as ordinary "thinking" or "knowing."

Thinking or knowing are complex "activities." We can distinguish at least two types of mentation on which we lean heavily in our efforts to organize or to manipulate the world conceptually. The first consists of the formation of a body of common-sense knowledge learned by experience or secondhand, that enables us to deal with life on terms of familiarity. This common-sense organization of thought, by which we "know" that stones fall and trees grow, forms the basis for those more abstract conventions and conjectures to which we give the philosophic names of causality, chance, identity, and the like.

This mode of mentation is indispensable for our ability to live in the world, or to "explain" it to ourselves or others. Yet we know very little about the process of gaining this kind of knowledge, save that it is accumulated slowly and painfully. Moreover, for all the power that common-sense knowledge exercises over our thought, we also know from intercultural comparisons that "common-sense" explanations of events differ widely from one culture to another, and that the world can have many different "natural" or "self-evident" appearances.

Common-sense generalization, acquired in the universal process of socialization, is not, however, the only process of apprehension on which we depend.

There is also a powerful kind of mental activity that "obeys" those rules of syntax and word sequence we call logic. When we perform the activity we call thinking, we frequently have recourse to these rules that define for us which sequences of utterance are legitimate or right, and which are illegitimate or wrong.

As Piaget has shown with his ingenious experiments, these formal logical steps have also to be learned.[13] The child does not know that the whole is equal to the sum of the parts, or that A must be bigger than C if it is bigger than B and if B is bigger than C. Such relationships are learned, often with great effort, and in some cases poorly: we all know people who cannot think "logically."

Now what is interesting about logical thought—which need not be Aristotelian logic—is that, once having been mastered, its rules master us. Having learned the rules of identity or transitivity, it is impossible to disavow them. Indeed, it is much easier to lie—to distort deliberately what one hears or sees—than to forswear the veracity of a proper syllogism. Since this logic has to be learned, as we have just said, we can only suppose that in some manner the rules of logic reflect the manner in which most adult minds "work."

Together, the common-sense organization of data and the obedience to canonical or logical rules of utterance describe a great deal of the activity we call rational discourse. They do not, however, embrace all our mental activities. Another, very important kind is our ability to perform such mental feats as suddenly "seeing the

[13]Jean Piaget, *The Construction of Reality in the Child* (New York: Basic Books, 1954).

point'' of something (what the psychologists call the "aha!" sensation), or discerning patterns, resemblances, or other relationships that are not discoverable by common sense or by formally structured logic.

Such insights, metaphors, associations, flights of fancy and the like impart a vast energy to psychic life. Indeed, I would venture that all that is "creative"—all that is a departure from received ideas or utterances—derives from this universally shared capability. Our ability to organize data into generalizations does not lead to novel ideas, but tends to solidify and routinize past experience; our pursuit of logic is, by definition, bounded by the rules that imperiously exert their sway. In sharp contrast, every novel conception or generalization, every invention of a new rule for logic, every new "image" of thought, we owe to the mysterious psychic process that accompany, but are distinct from discursive thought. Metaphors and images and insights bubble up "from below." We have no control over their generation or their acuity, whereas we do not feel so much at the mercy of uncontrollable forces when we try to think in common sense or formal ways. Imagination takes us by surprise, in a manner that cannot ordinarily be said of thinking.[14]

I have taken this detour because I believe that formal dialectics, in all its different forms, is an effort to capture and to reduce to communicable discourse this inventive psychic capacity. The elusive psychic

[14]Cf., Karl Popper, *The Logic of Scientific Discovery* (New York: Basic Books, 1959), p. 32: "My view [is] that every discovery contains an 'irrational element' or a 'creative intuition,' in Bergson's sense. . . ." For a searching treatment of the psychic processes underlying metaphor, see Stanley Burnshaw, *The Seamless Web* (New York: George Braziller, 1970), Chapter 3.

abilities we have discussed probably derive their energies from unconscious and preconscious processes of the mind. But it is not their origins about which I wish to speculate in these last pages, but rather their ramifications in the dialectical views that we have examined.

The connections are, I believe, twofold. First, much "creative" thought hinges on the possibility of discovering analogies, linkages, syntheses and the like between hitherto separated entities. This mental act of "leaping" from one thought to another has an obvious analogue to the idea of relationship, so central to dialectical philosophy.

Second, unlike common sense or logic, intuitive thought (to give a name to the spectrum of imaginative psychic activities) is often ambiguous and "contradictory." Freud, for example, remarks that symbols emerging from the unconscious are laden with ambivalent meanings—love and hate, male and female, etc. Here, as in dialectics, ambivalence refers to "unities" that can only be understood by the interpenetration and support of mutually exclusive concepts. (Freud also remarked on the tendency of certain words to possess contradictory meanings: "Cleave," for example, means both to sunder and to cling.)

The hypothesis, then, is that dialectics is at bottom an effort to systematize, or to translate into the realm of manageable, communicable thought, certain unconscious or preconscious modes of apprehending reality, especially social reality. This hypothesis gives us some clue as to why the exposition of dialectics leaves us satisfied at one level of our minds while dissatisfied at another. Its ideas of flux, contradiction, essence, remain elusive in terms of ordinary reasoned discourse.[15] Worse, the attempt to translate these terms into the structures of ordinary exposition either desiccates them—reducing dialectics to a set of definitions that can be riddled by the application of common sense or logic—or indicates their nondiscursive meaning by an allusive use of words, by recondite vocabularies, by italics that inject a suggestive tone of voice into prose, etc. Ambiguity, the bane of positivism, is the very essence of dialectics.

The result is the blurred and imprecise exposition—blurred and imprecise according to the criteria of common sense or logic—that caused Pareto to remark in exasperation that Marx's words were like bats: to some, mice; to others, birds. This is a statement that Bertell Ollman, who has strongly emphasized the relational core of dialectics, has called a profound insight into the truth.[16]

The same nondiscursive aspect of dialectics accounts, I suspect, for the extraordinary difficulties in communication that have been manifest among writers in this mode. The straightforward transmission of thought is encumbered by a seemingly inescapable tendency to obscurity and indirection. Finally, in the hands of less skilled writers it has produced that disorderly use of words and that talismanic resort to special vocabularies that has made of "dialectics" an excuse

---

[15]The previously cited example of Mandel (see Note 8 in this chapter) is a case in point. Mandel chastizes the Soviet theorist Smirnov for a definition of method that, in Mandel's words, "fails to take into account the crucial mediation between essence and appearance and thus reduces the problem to a confrontation of theory and empirical matter" op. cit., p. 17, n. 16). But how is one to know what is appearance and what is essence? To this question Mandel offers no answer because, I believe, there *is* no answer, any more than there is an answer to the question: "How should I think creatively?"

[16]Bertell Ollman, *Alienation, Marx's Conception of Man in Capitalist Society* (New York: Cambridge University Press, 1971, 1976), p. 3.

for bad thought or a cheap warrant of Marxist identity.

This nondiscursive capacity of mind from which I believe dialectics draws its strength poses a genuine difficulty for Marxism. The difficulty is that the very elements that generate clear communication in ordindary discourse—the relatively clear-cut languages of common sense and logic—are ill-qualified for the presentation of a dialectical view with its focus on the ideas of flux, contradiction, interpretation, etc. The result is a disturbing choice. To use the language of discursive thought (that is, the language built on empirical generalizations and logic) is to use a language that rules out the very ambiguities, Januslike meanings, and metaphorical referents that are the *raisons d'être* for a dialectical view. Dialectics seeks to tap levels of awareness that defy the syntaxes of common sense and logic. To present dialectics as a set of generalizations derived from empirical observation, or as an exercise in logic, is to betray the very purpose for which dialectics exists.

On the other hand, to eschew the language of reasoned discourse confines dialectics to the realm of statements for which no rules of procedure can be found. Dialectical statements may be as valid or important as those of common sense or logic, but their meanings are poorly communicated at the level of what we call rational explanation. From this deep-seated and far-reaching difficulty, I do not believe there is an escape. The perspective of dialectics imparts insights and perceptions to Marxism, but these gifts are, by the nature of the psychic processes to which they owe their existence, resistant to examination by the conventional modes of rational thought.

THREE

The Materialist Interpretation of History

MARXISM, AS WE have come to see, reflects a particular philosophic stance. But the pursuit of philosophy was never a central task either for Marx or most of his followers. The focal problem has always been the analysis of capitalism, the social order that presented Marx with an endlessly fascinating enigma that demanded understanding, as the unconscious was to present itself to Freud, and the very act of philosophizing to Plato.

Yet it would be an error to proceed directly from our philosophic inquiry to an examination of what Marx had to say about capitalism. Marx's socioanalysis tries to penetrate the surface appearances of the system and to unveil its concealed essence. We will retrace this task in our next chapter. But the key to Marx's penetrative insight lies elsewhere, in his perception that the concealed essence of capitalism is its own forgotten past, its long-disappeared history, preserved in disguise within its existing institutions and beliefs. History thereby becomes the entree for the Marxist study of capitalism, not merely to retrace its emergence from prior societies—a task we will not attempt in this book—but to open a perspective without which we cannot understand what capitalism is.[1]

This special historical vantage point is called the materialist interpretation of history, an interpretation that Marx described as follows:

The general result at which I arrived . . . can be briefly formulated as follows: In the social production of their life, men enter into definite relations that are indispensable and independent of their will, relations of production which correspond to a definite stage of development of their material productive forces. The sum total of these relations of production constitutes the economic structure of society, on which rises a legal and political superstructure and to which correspond definite forms of social consciousness. *The mode of production of material life conditions the social, political, and intellectual life process in general.* It is not the consciousness of men that determines their being, but, on the contrary, their social being that determines their consciousness.[2]

[1]The problem of selecting examples of Marxist historiography is necessarily invidious, but some examples are needed to give substance to the arguments that follow. I therefore offer the following selections as embodying some or all of the strengths and weaknesses that I shall stress. First, there are the historical writings of Marx himself, including not only his famous narrative and analytic essays on "The 18th Brumaire of Louis Napoleon," "The Civil War in France" (and many others), but the historical material integrally woven into the theoretic argument of *Capital*, especially Volume I, Part Eight, "On the So-Called Primitive Accumulation." A list of major works in the Marxist tradition must include Trotsky's *The Russian Revolution*. Modern history includes innumerable works written from a Marxist view. I will limit myself to mentioning a few authors, rather than itemizing their works: Perry Anderson, Eugene Genovese, Christopher Hill, Eric Hobsbawm, E.P. Thompson. The list could be much longer, but it will suffice to identify a body of work that is readily available.

[2]My italics. From the *Preface to a Contribution to the Critique of Political Economy*, in *The Marx-Engels Reader* 2nd ed., ed. Robert C. Tucker, (New York: Norton, 1978), p. 4.

We obtain a sharp first impression of this materialist view by comparing it with its opposite, an idealist view. In the eyes of an idealist such as Hegel, history appears altogether differently from the way it appears to Marx. It is not material life, but thought that gives to history its meaning, its intelligibility, its shaping force, its "essence." From such a perspective, ideas "create" history and determine its form, and history itself—that is, the human narrative—must be seen as the embodiment of ideas realized in events.

For Marx it is just the other way around, which is why he claimed to have stood Hegel on his feet. In Marx's view, that which gives meaning, intelligibility, thrust and essence to history is the actual engagement of men and women with their material circumstances, above all with the ever-present necessity to recreate the material requirements of their own continuance. From such a materialist angle, ideas are anchored in, rather than existing independently of, the material setting of history. However much these ideas may act on and shape the material setting, they must in the first instance be produced within it, and must in some general sense be compatible with it.

This raises an immediate problem. Does the materialist interpretation, with its emphasis on production, reduce all of history to an economic determinism? What does Engels mean when he writes in *Anti-Dühring* that ". . . the ultimate causes of all social changes and political revolutions are to be sought, not in the minds of men, in their increasing insight into eternal

63

truth and justice, but in changes in the mode of production and exchange; they are to be sought not in the *philosophy* but in the *economics* of the epoch concerned."[3]

As we shall see, there are very difficult questions associated with the notion that economics is the engine of history—not only difficulties in determining the precise degree of influence to be accorded to economic activities, but difficulties in defining exactly what activities are to be designated as "economic". It will best serve our purposes, however, if we lay these matters aside for the moment, and seek to understand the materialist view by first investigating the central idea used by Marx and Engels to organize their study of history: the idea of a *mode of production*.

A mode of production is not a simple concept. It is used in the first instance to identify and separate clearly different social forms of production and distribution: thus Marx speaks of an Asiatic mode of production, a slave mode, a feudal mode, a capitalist mode, and so on. Thus one meaning of a mode of production is simply a compartmentalization of history that uses as its main criterion different systems of organizing economic, rather than political or religious, life.

Of greater interest is the *internal* construction of these modes. For a common dichotomous aspect applies to all modes of production, however different they may be in other regards. One of these two internal divisions Marx calls the *forces of production*, referring to socie-

[3]From *A Handbook of Marxism*, ed. E. Burns, (New York: Random House, 1935), p. 279. Engels's italics.

ty's means of material reproduction—its population, skills, arts, techniques, and artifacts. The other constituent, equally important in the ongoing process of productive activity, is denoted the *relations of production*. This refers to the social arrangements that direct the forces of production and that allocate its output. Here are the institutions of power and hierarchy, embodied in the social classes that we find in all modes of production. These classes are largely defined by the common relationships of their members to the productive and distributive process (lords, serfs, wage-earners, capitalists, etc.), and are characterized by the unequal, and usually antagonistic, relationship that these classes bear to one another.

It can be seen that neither the forces nor the relations of production are narrowly economic concepts. The forces of production embody the skills and arts of the population and are thereby inextricably mixed with its cultural and technical heritage. The relations of production necessarily embrace the legal and political and social bonds that legitimate and enforce the roles of the different classes. Thus political and social, even religious, elements pervade the economic elements. If, then, the entire mode of production gives an "economic" cast to the materialist view of history, it is because it is organized around the overriding necessity of production, not because economic *motives*, as such, are presumed to dominate all others, or because economic *activities*, such as buying or selling, are supposed directly to dictate what men and women will think.

A letter written by Engels in 1890 sheds light on Marx's and his own conception of this issue:

> According to the materialist conception of history, the *ultimately* determining element in history is the production and reproduction of real life. More than this neither Marx nor I have ever asserted. Hence if anybody twists this into saying that the economic element is the *only* determining one, he transforms that proposition into a meaningless, abstract, senseless phrase. The economic situation is the basis, but the various elements of the superstructure: political forms of the class struggle and its results, to wit: constitutions established by the victorious class after a successful battle, etc., juridical forms, and then even the reflexes of all these actual struggles in the brains of the participants, political, juristic, philosophical theories, religious views and their further development into systems of dogmas, all also exercise their influence upon the course of the historical struggles, and in many cases preponderate in determining their *form*. . . . Marx and I are ourselves partly to blame for the fact that the younger people sometimes lay more stress on the economic side than is due to it. We had to emphasize the main principle *vis-à-vis* our adversaries, who denied it, and we had not always the time, the place, or the opportunity to allow the other elements involved in the interaction to come into their rights.[4]

The crude "economism" that on occasion has marked Marxist historiography is not, therefore, inherent in its materialist emphasis. What Marx called the economic "base" is conceived as setting *limits* for the kind of sociopolitical arrangements that are compatible with survival—a hunting society will not be able to function with the "superstructure" of a commercial

[4]From Robert C. Tucker, *The Marx-Engels Reader*, pp. 760, 762.

society and vice versa—but a given foundation can underpin numerous variations of the superstructural elements. The mode of production, which describes the way in which social reproduction is assured, thereby helps us understand the prevailing direction of the arrows of causation within society, without imposing a rigid or deterministic relationship of "economic" cause and "social" effect. I do not think, for example, that any Marxist today would argue that the state is just an instrument of the ruling class. On the other hand, all Marxists would claim that the state is generally used to defend the interests of the ruling class. It is this latter view to which non-Marxist history tends to be blind, and it is in that sense that "economic determinism" plays its influential role.[5]

(2)

Materialism in itself, however, does not suffice to identify the Marxist perspective. Adam Smith, for example, adopted an essentially materialist viewpoint in his theory of four historic "stages" of history— hunting, pastoralism, settled agriculture, and commercial society—in which the underlying method of organizing economic life determined the appropriate form of government and property relations.[6] That which

[5]I do not wish to leave the impression that there are no definitional or other problems connected with the ideas of the forces and relations of production, or with the larger concept of a mode of production. Controversy abounds within the Marxist literature as to the internal consistency, or even as to the legitimacy, of all these terms. Their usage by historians varies considerably. Nonetheless, I think there is a widespread—although not unanimous—acceptance of their meaning and roles, which I have indicated here.

[6]See Adam Smith, *Lectures on Justice, Police, Revenue and Arms* (New York: August Kelley, 1964), pp. 14–16, and *Wealth of Nations* (New York: Random House, 1937), pp. 653, 669–74.

gives Marxist historiography its distinctive character is the fusion of a materialist starting point with a dialectical conception of the processes of historical change. That is why, despite the fact that Marx himself never used the phrase, Marxist history has come to be called "dialectical materialism."

The dialectical element within the materialist vision of history emerges from an attribute of the mode of production to which we have not yet paid due notice. This is the relationship of extreme tension resulting from the unequal relations between the superior and inferior classes within any mode. The inequality may take many forms, but it is usually evidenced by the vastly disproportionate access to, or ownership of, wealth that is the prerogative of the ruling class.

From this systemic fact of inequality arises the main driving force of historical change: the *class struggle* through which the existing division of wealth and privilege is attacked by those who are its sufferers and defended by those who are its beneficiaries. Occasionally the struggle is visible as a slave revolt or a peasant uprising. More often it is waged in muted contests over legal entitlements or economic prerogatives. It may indeed be almost completely disguised in the form of battles of ideas, or political or religious disputes, in which the immediate matters under debate conceal, even from the protagonists themselves, the underlying theme of class opposition.

The idea of class struggle is associated with a dialectical view because it reveals a contraction located within all modes of production. This contradiction involves the interaction between the forces of production and the relations of production. The forces of production require the *cooperation* of the main classes so that material existence can be renewed and sustained. The relations of production reflect the class *antagonisms* we have just described. Thus society reproduces itself, but only under conditions of tension that threaten to disrupt its socioeconomic structure. Therefore, when Marx and Engels write in the *Manifesto* that "the history of all heretofore existing societies is the history of class struggles," they are not merely describing a train of dramatic events in history, but identifying a dialectical process that gives penetration to our understanding of history.

The inherent nature of class struggle is therefore the main theoretical insight that the dialectic imparts to history. It enables us to see that class struggle is rooted in the structural properties of a mode of production, and that it will appear—hidden or overt, focused on one kind of class privilege or another—in all modes. This antagonistic relationship is put under further tension by changes in the forces of production, technical or otherwise, that alter the tasks of different classes, and thus reopen the terms of their mutual dealings. But it would exist, in any case, as a "unity of opposites" that must be sustained to assure the continuity of the mode of production itself.

This insight is the main *aperçu* that Marxist history gives us for the socioanalysis of capitalism. For we can now see that a struggle must exist within capitalism, regardless of the accidents of history or the heartlessness or stupidity of capitalist classes. Although the form and intensity of the struggle may vary widely from one capitalist society to another, from the Marxist view the struggle will be as inescapable and integral a part of all such societies as are the class differences on which they rest.

We will examine this concept more critically later in this chapter. But first we should take note of a second, more muted dialectical theme that also gives its distinguishing character to Marxist history. This is another contradiction-laden process, related to but separate from that of class struggle, to be found in the peculiar human condition Marx calls *alienation*. Alienation is a condition of social and psychological deformation through which humanity passes as a consequence of its historic experience—a passage that begins when mankind moves from its earliest "history-less" beginnings into the overwhelming stream of experience that we call history, and from which it will emerge only when humanity finally leaves that stream by learning to control its own destiny.

The historical drama of alienation begins in the state of *primitive communism*, the name given by Marx and Engels to the social organization of primitive peoples. In these societies, the class divisions of later civilizations are not to be found. Property is almost nonexistent, save for minor personal belongings. There is almost no formal apparatus of government. Nothing like the state exists. The economic basis of society— usually hunting or gathering or primitive agriculture—

is seamlessly woven into its social and political functions. The division of labor plays only a small part in the organization of production. Conflicts and perhaps contradictions may exist in such societies, but they cannot arise from the conditions, nor assume the forms, characteristic of later socioeconomic formations.

In this primal setting man exists in a highly socialized condition that Marx calls *"a generic being, a tribal being, a herd animal."* [7] This condition is not meant to be glorified. Primitive communism is not a Garden of Eden. On the contrary, humanity at this stage is not only threatened by extinction from natural causes, but is beset by the terrors of the unknown. The simple life does not bring forth a surplus of material goods above that needed for mere existence. Neither material advance, nor intellectual progress is in evidence. Primitive culture persists, but it does not evolve.

Marxist history gives us no special explanation as to why or how the static cultures of primitive communism are disrupted. It only notes that as these cultures give way, we encounter civilizations in which the dominant features are precisely those which are absent from primitive society. In ancient Asia, Egypt, Greece, Rome, Africa—in short, wherever civilizations have arisen—class structures quickly appear. Property becomes a massive social consideration, although not the kind of property characteristic of capitalist societies. Governments and states emerge. The economic basis of

[7] E. Hobsbawm, ed., *Pre-Capitalist Economic Formations* (New York: International Publishers, 1965), p. 96. Marx's italics.

life turns toward advanced agriculture, commerce, and to a greater or lesser degree, industry. The division of labor becomes a necessary and ubiquitous feature of economic life.

With the appearance of class-stratified, state-dominated, labor-specialized society, the condition of man changes dramatically. The subsistence economies of the past give way to surplus-generating societies capable of creating extraordinary collective achievements—Great Walls and pyramids, irrigation systems, temples. Elaborate intellectual achievements in astronomy, law, literature, and religion rival the material advances of their cultures.

But human existence loses its unity and wholeness before the division of class domination and over-specialized social function. The working person becomes separated from the product of his own labor. His work, once the very expression and incorporation of his generic being, now confronts him as a thing apart, indeed as a thing that commands him as property. Marx calls this subordination of the worker to the "reified" product of his labor, confronting him as an alien thing, *alienation*. Although it exists in other kinds of societies, it attains its most complete expression in the regime of capitalism where, as we will see in our next chapter, alienated labor assumes the form of capital.

The theme of alienation has many obvious parallels and cross relations with that of class struggle. Both are dialectical processes; class struggle as the contradiction imposed by the functioning of a mode of production, alienation as that imposed by the process of material advancement.[8] But what is perhaps most striking of all is a parallel of another kind. This is the transcendent thrust displayed by both.

For the Marxist depiction of class struggle is not merely that of a never-ending contest that will continue as long as mankind exists. Rather, it is a struggle that eventually achieves the conditions necessary for its own resolution. In the mode of production of capitalism, class antagonisms are finally simplified to two great opposing camps—workers and owners, proletarians and capitalists. The class struggle under capitalism thus leads to the possibility of a final victory by the great masses of individuals who will create a "dictatorship of the proletariat" (words that have since haunted Marxists, but that were not intended by Marx to imply a tyrannical rule). The dictatorship of the proletariat would establish the hegemony of the masses, the domination by the previously dominated. The vanquished class would be absorbed and disappear. A terminus of history would be reached in which a classless society would vindicate the long historical struggle.[9]

[8]For a description of alienation from a dialectical standpoint, see Bertell Ollman, *Alienation, Marx's Conception of Man in Capitalist Society,* especially pp. 135–136. The process that I have described above bears obvious parallels to Freud's contradiction-laden depiction of the civilizational malaise in *Civilization and its Discontents,* save that Freud offers no hope of an ultimate transcendence of the neurotic condition, whereas Marx implies such a hope for alienation.

[9]Perhaps the most direct expression of this view is to be found in a letter written by Marx in 1852 to his friend Joseph Wedemeyer: "Long before me' bourgeois historians had described the historical development of [the] class struggle. . . . What I did that was new was to prove: 1) that the *existence of classes* is only bound up with *particular historical phases of the development of production,* 2) that the class struggle necessarily leads to the *dictatorship of the proletariat,* 3) that this dictatorship itself only constitutes the transition to the *abolition of all classes* and to *a classless society."* Marx's italics. From Robert C. Tucker, *The Marx-Engels Reader,* p. 220.

A similar hope-filled conclusion may await the drama of alienation. Here we must extrapolate Marx's thought, for his comments on the promise of communism are very few, as we shall see in Chapter V. But the extrapolation seems justified. Once again capitalism plays the critical role. For under capitalism the forces of production are finally developed to enormous heights, making it possible for the first time to release mankind from the indentured servitude it has been forced to accept as the price for material advance. In the final stages of Marx's conception of capitalism, its contradictions intensify until its integument, in the famous phrase, bursts asunder. Less trumpeted, but also implicit in this cataclysmic change is "humanity's leap from the realm of necessity into the realm of freedom," in Engel's equally notable phrase in his tract *Anti-Dühring*. Mankind at long last transcends not only its thralldom to the social domination of an oppressive minority, but its dehumanization in the quintessentially human act of work. Thus Marxist history ultimately points to a double victory for mankind—a victory over the domination of class rule and a victory over the deformation of alienation.

(3)

Problems abound in this epic conception of history, but I think we should begin by emphasizing its formidable strengths. Here I would place first the leverage given to historical investigation by the adoption of a materialist view. This is not to state, of course, that only from such a perspective can one write good history, or that this perspective unfailingly serves the historian's needs. The perspective is more useful for some periods and for some questions than for others.[10] But an organizing principle of great power emerges from this vantage that is largely absent from other views. This is the emphasis on class struggle, with its focus on the roles, fortunes, and motives of social classes as the red thread of social history.

The theme of class struggle tends to be ignored, glossed over, or denied by many non-Marxist historians—above all when their investigations concern contemporary society. Yet, I find the theme both valid and instructive. There can hardly be a demurrer against the Marxist contention that gross class differences are visible in all socioeconomic formations. The division of wealth and power among social classes, in all societies above the very simplest, displays extreme and systematic inequalities, a fact as true of contemporary advanced capitalist societies (although to a lesser degree) as it was true of societies of feudal or despotic lineage. The disagreement among historians can only arise as to the importance of these differences, and the presence or absence of a "struggle" to resolve them.

Here much of the difficulty is that one imagines class struggle as overt or violent. In fact, however, it is usually latent rather than manifest, potential rather than actual. In most societies the inequalities of class position are obscured or minimized or rationalized—an attitude often fervently supported by the underclasses

---

[10]See, Georg Lukács, "The Changing Function of Historical Materialism," *History and Class Consciousness*, (Cambridge, M.I.T. Press, 1971), p. 238.

themselves. Thus a Marxist perspective is of necessity as much interested in centripetal and legitimating social institutions and structures as in centrifugal and disruptive ones. In fact, the need to search for mechanisms that bestow social harmony is emphasized from a Marxist viewpoint, precisely because Marxism, unlike conventional social science, does not hold that harmony is a natural condition for a social order.

The theme of class struggle is therefore powerful because it directs attention to a kind of "secret history"—a history of social activity and ideology of which the protagonists themselves may be unaware. Such central institutions as the military, the law, the schools, and the church come under a scrutiny they would otherwise escape, as participants, willy-nilly, in a struggle to sustain or tear down a given distribution of social rights. In the class struggle, these central institutions are usually to be found on the side of the dominant classes, although they may occasionally play a role in redefining or even in opposing their hegemony.

The determinative role of class struggle in history is a matter open to argument. The essential contention of Marxism is that the struggle is of such intensity and pervasive influence that it colors, either subtly or crassly, the ideas and beliefs of even the most sheltered activities. From this premise, not only social thought and political activity, but art, literature, religion, and philosophy must bear the telltale marks of having been produced in a society that is consciously and unconsciously engaged in a silent, suppressed struggle from which none are exempt and in which all must choose sides. All ideational activity, therefore, must reveal on its surface or in its depths the polarizing effects of this historic condition of riven social life. A main task of the historian is to search out and identify the overt or hidden presence of this materialist influence.

This is, I think, a defensible, and certainly a richly suggestive view. I need hardly add that it can easily be abused. A reflexive accusation of "class interest" can obscure or distort our comprehension of the idea itself. Marxist history of this kind is as bad as history that stubbornly refuses to recognize any motive of class interest. But it would be foolish to fight out the issue on these grounds. The importance to be accorded to the theme of class struggle is best left open, to be determined and demonstrated in each case, rather than assumed a priori. From such an approach, the materialist "interpretation" of history becomes a rich hypothesis, rather than a determination emptied of significance by having been decided in advance; an interpretation that emerges from the subject, rather than one thrust upon it.

A second source of strength for Marxist historiography lies in its emphasis on dialectics—its insistence that history is not only conflict-laden, but *inherently* conflict-laden, and that its conflictual elements yield their meanings only when we understand them as "contradictions" within a dialectical framework.

Before looking critically at this idea, it is necessary to appreciate its importance. The idea of contradiction, as we have seen, is that social systems may display tendencies that are both necessary for their existence and yet incompatible with it. Such a conception provides a unifying overview with respect to many eras of historic change that otherwise appear only chaotic or patternless. Prime examples of this are the dually destructive and constructive roles of the merchant class during the evolution of feudalism, or the similar roles played by the capitalist class in the process of capitalist development itself. An awareness of dialectical change, embodied in the idea of contradiction, thereby opens another "secret history" of great elucidating significance.[11]

No less important, a dialectical perspective is valuable because it tends to make its practitioners conscious of their philosophical premises. Conventional history does not, as a rule, declare its philosophic bias. This means, since one cannot write history without ideas as to what is true and false, believable and not believable, that history tends to accept the contemporary, established philosophic tenets of positivism, with their stress on empirical findings and testable propositions.

Positivism is a formidable tool in historical, as well as scientific, work. It provides us with an immensely useful—if sometimes elusive—line of demarcation between scientific (testable, empirical) propositions and "metaphysical" (nontestable, nonempirical) ones. But positivism also has severe limitations as a guide for

[11]Many historians have understood the roles of "creative destruction" exercised by various classes within their historical epochs. That which divides the Marxist from the non-Marxist appreciation of these roles in their explicit interpretation by Marxists as embodying "contradictions," not merely conflicts. In so doing, Marxists emphasize the immanent, intrinsic nature of these conflicts within the "unity" of the socioeconomic formations in which they appear.

historical investigation. For the historian's task is not just that of selecting and testing "facts," but of establishing the boundaries of facts and their embeddedness in a contextual situation.[12] History without "interpretation" has come to be seen as a self-deceptive undertaking, the naïve assertion that facts speak for "themselves," not for their selector. But it follows that positivism is also saddled with the problem of interpretation; namely, its acquiescence before whatever viewpoint establishes its facts. Thus the positivist does not avoid the problems of interpretation. He merely smuggles them undeclared through the customs house.

A dialectical approach, by contrast, is always self-consciously interpretational, because its concern for "essence"—rather than facts—forces it to confront the ambiguous, many-layered, context of events. Contradictions do not present themselves in any pure form; they must be *discovered* within the flux of many conflictive events. The consequent interpretations of a Marxist historian may be inadequate or simply wrong, but at least the crucial task is directly visible, rather than being allowed to exert its influence in unrecognized ways.

One last advantage of the Marxist approach to history must now be given its due. This is its fusion of theory and practice, contemplation and intervention, observation and interposition. This is perhaps the proudest boast of Marxism in general, as well as of Marxist

---

[12]See *Critical Sociology*, ed. Paul Connerton (New York: Penguin, 1976), Part II (The Hermeneutic Tradition), especially essays by Dilthey, Gadamer, Lorenzer, Taylor, and Ricoeur.

historiography in particular. Marxism is intended to provide more than an understanding of history. It is intended to serve as a guide for making history.

Toward this end, the philosophic, historic, economic, and other theoretical productions of Marxism are each meant to serve a double purpose. By illumining the past, they enlighten mankind as to its heritage: they reveal elements of history congealed in the present; they open consciousness to wholly unsuspected aspects of social existence. Thus, they change the terms by which we accept the present, and thereby change our ability to shape the future. The unity of theory and practice—of knowledge and action—is not, therefore, intended to be a forced unification of two intrinsically different activities; instead, it recognizes that thought and action are inseparably bonded in the experience of life itself. Thought provides the understanding of the past by which we guide our actions, action expresses the translation of thought into our engagement with the future.

Of course, such a unification also imports enormous perils into the making of history, perils monstrously evident in the way "Marxist" theory has been used to justify cruel and inhuman actions. That is a matter to which we shall return. Yet the idea of a unity of theory and practice is a laudable one, however much that idea may have been abused in actuality—we are reminded here again of the parallel experiences of Marxism and Christianity.

The laudable element in Marxism is its declaration that the only "meaning" to be ascribed to history is its moral unfolding, or more precisely, its orientation to human freedom. We must not forget that Marxism itself springs from the passionate and unrestrained commitment of Karl Marx to the idea of human emancipation, not to mere inquiry for inquiry's sake.[13] That moral fervor continues to animate Marxist historiography. This is in contrast with the studied efforts of many conventional historians to detach themselves from the "value judgments" that will presumably impair the worth of their findings.

I will not waste time in acknowledging the need for standards of professional discipline applicable to all historical work, Marxist and non-Marxist alike. But the commitment of Marxism to the cause of human freedom, however much it may open the way to the evils of a self-justifying religiosity, strikes me as an indispensable dimension for the study of history. That moral fervor can lead to evil is a fact demonstrated centuries before Marxism was invented. Marxism is not alone in posing that risk. It is alone, however, in its effort to construct a vision of historical progress, culminating in the idea of a classless and unalienated society. The vision is also alone in its insistence that mankind makes its own history, and thereby makes itself—not just as it pleases, as Marx remarks, but nonetheless wholly by its own efforts. No other study of history is so consciously oriented to mastering history, as is Marxism. For that reason alone it warrants our respect.

[13]For a study of Marx's political orientation, see Hal Draper, *Karl Marx's Theory of Revolution* (New York: Monthly Review Press, 1978, 1979).

(4)

The insights provided by a materialist view of history and by a search for contradictions within the historic process are so compelling that some elements of Marxism have by now penetrated into much conventional historiography, just as a Freudian interpretation of behavior has tinctured much "non-Freudian" psychology. It would be wrong, however, to conclude this résumé without paying careful heed to Marxism's shortcomings; there is an *against* as well as a *for* with respect to Marxist history. Some of its difficulties have already been noted; here I should like to emphasize others of a still more deep-reaching kind.

Let us begin with materialism. According to the materialist view, the key to the course of history lies in the ultimate, dominating influence of mankind's productive activities. We have already taken note of the need to avoid picturing this as a crude "economism," in which a materialist base dominates and wholly determines an ideational superstructure. But that is not the most difficult problem that materialism poses. The challenge, rather, lies in defining the material sphere itself without introducing elements of idealism; or, if you will, in distinguishing activities in the base from those in the superstructure.

Presumably the base of society, where its material forces are to be found, comprises those activities necessary to assure its physical survival and reproduction. Here, of course, we find its economic life, above all the continuous production and distribution of the material output by which it is sustained. The question, however, is whether these activities could assure social continuance without the support of other noneconomic activities. A host of actions that are not "economic" by any conventional definition must be performed if the economic base is to operate. Children must be reared. Some kind of law and order must prevail. Disputes must be adjudicated. In short, as Gordon Leff has written, "There cannot be activity as between men unless there is a social cement that binds them; and this is as much political, legal and moral as it is economic."[14]

These noneconomic activities must no doubt be consonant with certain basic constraints established by the general forces of production: an industrial nation cannot rear its children like a tribe of hunters. But such constraints are so wide as to be of little use for historical analysis. Societies with similar economic bases have displayed striking differences in their political and cultural developments, as the most cursory consideration of the histories of capitalist states makes clear. In addition, the rise and rivalries of nation-states—perhaps the central narrative of modern human history—is only partially and fitfully elucidated by developments in the "bases" of those societies.

I have not developed this argument in order once again to assert the inadequacy of an "economic interpretation" of history. The question, rather, is to know how widely the net must be cast to capture an

[14]Gordon Leff, *The Tyranny of Concepts* (London: Merlin Press, 1961), p. 114; see also Althusser, *Lenin and Philosophy* (New York: Monthly Review Press, 1971), pp. 127ff.

adequate economic interpretation of events. The inter-mingling of nonmaterial activities with material ones, the suffusion of ideational elements throughout the body of society, the inextricable unity of "social" and "economic" life, make it difficult to draw boundaries around the material sphere. The problem for a materialist version of history, therefore, is to take into account the influences of law and politics, religion and ideology, and other elements of the ideational realm, without losing the distinctive emphasis that is materialism's claim for superiority. This is not an impossible task, as witness the exemplars cited in the initial footnote to this chapter, but it is certainly not an easy one.[15]

Our second problem returns us once again to dialectics, a subject whose importance within Marxism becomes steadily larger as we penetrate more deeply. Here we must examine two difficulties.

The first is already familiar to us and can be quickly disposed of. It is the tendency to blur the distinction between a "conflict" and a "contradiction." Conflicts abound in history, as they do in nature (in the form of simple oppositions of forces). We do not require a Marxist perspective to recognize them. But for a con-

[15]In a famous letter to his friend Kugelman (*Letter to Kugelman*, [New York: International Publishers, 1934], p. 73), Marx claims that "every child" knows that a nation that stopped working could quickly cease to exist. But it is also true that a nation that stopped thinking, or that disregarded all Ten Commandments, would also soon cease to be a viable community. I might add that an exclusive focus on materialism involves us in precisely the dilemmas that a dialectical philosophy seeks to avert. See again Richard Norman, "On Dialectic," *Radical Philosophy*, no. 14, Summer 1976.

flict to merit designation as a contradiction, it must be embedded in the process of social change in a genuinely "contradictory" way. It must bind two antagonistic and incompatible processes into one conceptual unity.

In historiography, as in philosophy, to bestow this designation indiscriminately is to vitiate its force. It is one thing, therefore, to seek a materialist perspective on social change or on the dynamics of various socioeconomic formations, and it is another to label these changes as "dialectical" or "contradictory." *The collisions of history cannot always be dialectical, if we are to preserve an elucidating use for that word and not merely to employ it to indicate a universal, and therefore uninteresting, property of things.* Dialectics, like materialism, must remain a hypothesis, an intellectual problematic, not an assumption that would reduce it to the level of a tautology or a metaphysic. The careless use of its terms, in history as in philosophy, only impairs their power when correctly applied.

A second problem posed by dialectics has to do with a matter we have already noted in our examination of the ideas of class struggle and alienation; namely, the assumption that the dialectical processes underlying these themes of history would lead to their resolution in a *final* class struggle, ultimately overcoming the condition of alienated being.

At one level, of course, the problem is one of fact. Has the class struggle become simplified and sharpened as the dialectical sequence predicted? Is there, realistically, a prospect of a "realm of freedom" under socialism, whether we define that freedom in social or

85

political terms? The answer to these questions, to date, is clearly No. The temptation is therefore great to dismiss the entire dialectical scheme as falsified by events, or to relegate it to a mere statement of faith, perhaps of inspirational importance but of no scientific value. (There is, of course, a "defense" in the assertion that the resolutions will "eventually" or even "inevitably" occur in the future, but such a defense would today be regarded as a sign of weakness, not strength.)

I do not, however, want to dispose of the problem in this manner. Later we shall examine the prospects for class struggle and alienation. At this juncture, I wish to bring to the fore another answer to the charges brought against the dialectical interpretation of events. *The answer denies that a dialectical interpretation of history predicts any climactic or resolutive terminus at all.* All that dialectics gives us is an understanding of class struggle and alienation as intrinsic elements in the movement of societies through time. As to any "finality" to these movements, dialectics says nothing, even though Marx himself (and innumerable Marxists after him) believed in the impending end to class struggle and perhaps to alienation.

Yet this mode of "rescuing" the argument reveals a very important weakness within dialectics. For the rescue is not one that would be gratefully received by Marxists. As we have already noted, the vision of a dialectical history, *forever* engaged in internecine warfare, *forever* condemned to some condition of alienation, *never* achieving a transcendence over its historic burden, is one that would strike most Marxists as intolerable. The extreme discomfort that such a view instills reveals for my purposes the telltale weakness of the dialectical view. This is its tacit teleology, its unstated millennial assumptions. The Marxist view of history is not content to declare that ceaseless change is inherent in history as an aspect of the nature of all reality. It imposes a Design on the course of history, a design in no wise less idealist than the vast mystical resolution attributed to history by Hegel. A view of history as a pageant of ceaseless change without moral transcendence is not one that Marxists can accept. In the end it is Hegel who turns Marx upside down.[16]

Now to turn to the last of the problems associated with a Marxist view of history, a problem that emerges from its commitment to a unity of theory and practice. This is the problem of the relation between the masses of men and women by whose life activities *praxis* will be determined, and the handful of men and women in whose possession *theoria* is to be found.

Few questions have agitated Marxists more violently than the proper relation between thought and action. Opinions still range from the assumption that the

[16]I should add that it is possible to maintain that Marx had two conceptions of history, not one—a conception of "repetitive history" that did indeed forever reproduce a given society without any sense of transcendence, and a conception of "evolutionary history," of which capitalism is the main, and perhaps sole, example. To put it differently, one might claim that a Marxist view of history, up to the advent of feudalism in the West, is essentially random, devoid of any directional impetus; whereas from feudalism on, the movement of history takes on an "ineluctable" cast. In the latter case, the teleology of which I speak above is confined only to history from feudalism on. The criticism is unaffected by being confined to a smaller space of time. (For a discussion of the two modes of history, see Claude Lefort, "Marx: from One Vision of History to Another," *Social Research*, Winter 1978, especially p. 627.)

masses "know best" about the tactics and strategy of class struggle, to the view that the masses are unreliable and uninformed, and must depend on the guidance and enlightenment of a party elite.

The issue at stake is a profound one. If Marxist theory is believed capable of yielding "correct" insights into history's inner logic, a knowledge of this theory gives to its holders an unchallengeable right to determine action, as a physician may ruthlessly impose a painful treatment on the assumption that his is the only way to cure an ailment. On the other hand, if theory is admitted to fall short of certitude—if "correct" strategies cannot be deduced beforehand—then action becomes its own legitimation, and whatever treatment the physician imposes itself determines the diagnosis to be made of the patient's illness. In both cases, theory and practice are "united"; but in the first, action becomes the slave of theory, while in the second, theory is only an apology for action. To be sure, it is not only Marxist leaders who impose their wills in the name of some guiding idea, or who justify their decisions by rewriting their principles. But it is only for Marxists that a philosophic commitment to a "unity" of theory and practices elevates this question to one of central moral and intellectual importance.[17]

Is there a way of combining *theoria* and *praxis* that can utilize the search for scientific insight to inform, but never to dictate, action; and that can create for action the

[17]For an interesting discussion of the need for a reconsideration of the roles of theory and practice, see Perry Anderson, *Considerations on Western Marxism* (London: New Left Library, 1976), pp. 110, 111.

role of validating, but never of dominating, the task of theory? The question is more easily put than answered, and to date the Marxist response has been crude in political life and disappointing in intellectual formulation. Nevertheless, it is here that the political usefulness and the moral validity of the Marxist stance toward history will finally be determined.

FOUR

The Socioanalysis of Capitalism

AND SO WE arrive at the *raison d'être* for Marxism, as Marx himself saw it: to understand the mode of production called capitalism. All that has gone before in this book can be described as a mere explication of the premises from which Marx launched his life's project. All his dialectical insights and all his historical formulations were developed only as tools to be pressed into the service of his central, ever-present task, the most searching, exhaustive, and complete examination to which any form of socioeconomic organization has ever been subject.[1]

Marx set himself a specific historical objective in

[1]So central is the work of Marx to the analysis of capitalism that this chapter will be mainly devoted to an exposition of the main themes in *Capital* and, to a lesser extent, the *Grundrisse*. The additions of later scholars in the Marxist tradition will be identified as they are introduced.

One further point should be made here. Marx's *Capital,* as vast as it is, constitutes only a small portion of his intended project. The works we possess examine "capital in general," but we know from the *Grundrisse* that Marx's intention was to treat in detail the questions of the state, international trade, and the international market. In a personal commentary on this chapter Ronald Blackwell writes: "I regard it as one of the major failures of 'Marxism' that it has never attempted to complete the system along the lines indicated by Marx, but rather has sought to apply—usually with considerable violence to the possibility of understanding—the most abstract propositions of this discourse *immediately* to economic life—what Marx described as "forced abstraction." This is as true of Luxemburg, Hilferding, and Bukharin, as it is of lesser Marxists. This immediate contrast of abstract determination and phenomena—insofar as it disregards inter-

this task, namely, to discover the "laws of motion" inherent within the capitalist mode of production. This objective, manifested in Marx's explorations or prognoses of various tendencies of the system, including its ever-sharpening contradictions and class conflicts, has won for Marx his greatest fame and his strongest criticism. Yet, to my mind, his prognostications are not so remarkable, nor even so "Marxist," as another aspect of his investigations to which much less attention is usually paid: his exposure of the capitalist mode to that penetrative criticism I have called socioanalysis—the historically oriented, dialectically based dissection of the particular institutions and beliefs of capitalism.

For it is from the hidden essence of capitalism, as we shall see, that its motions emerge. This socioanalytic aspect of Marx's work, with which the present chapter will be mainly concerned, is what I believe to be his most important and enduring contribution to the understanding of capitalism. I will, of course, discuss the famous laws of motion, for and against. But I must confess that I am entirely "for" the socioanalytic import of Marx's work, as I am unreservedly for the penetrative achievements of Freud and Plato. To put it baldly, I find it imaginable, although unlikely, that the

---

mediate determinations—has generated two opposite but equally deficient responses:

      a. empiricism/eclecticism—where the phenomena are grasped and theory "gives"; and

      b. dogmatism—where theory is grasped and phenomena are denied.

    Blackwell continues: "The correct response would be to develop the intermediate links on the basis of a careful study of both Marxian theory and the phenomena of economic life. Should it be impossible to develop such links, then the limits of this form of theoretical reflection would be established in a determinate way."

next century will declare Marx to have been completely mistaken as to the future course of capitalism; but as long as capitalism exists, I do not believe that we will ever be able to declare that he was mistaken in his identification of its inner nature.

(1)

Marx's view of capitalism is essentially historic, always on guard against temptations to depict the system in abstract terms that have no historical concreteness. Capitalism in his eyes is a stage and a staging ground in the long historic journey that we have previously described. Yet, to our surprise, his socioanalysis of the system does not begin with a description of its historic origins; in fact, this matter does not receive direct attention until the very end of Volume I of *Capital*. Instead, the examination begins with what appears at first sight to be an unremarkable aspect of the system, indeed its simplest and seemingly most understandable element. This is the everyday commodity, the individual good in which the wealth of the system is incorporated. As the first sentence of *Capital* reads: "The wealth of those societies in which the capitalist mode of production prevails, presents itself as an 'immense accumulation of commodities,' its unit being the single commodity."[2]

The choice of the commodity as the point of entry into capitalism seems odd. Why not the business enterprise, the locus of the distinctive form of productive

[2]The interior quotation is from Marx's previous essay, "A Contribution to the Critique of Political Economy."

activity in capitalism? Why not the marketplace, the social institution that organizes and colors so much of capitalist economic life? Why not an abstract model of the system as a whole, setting before our eyes the framework of ideas that would subsequently be demonstrated in detail?

The answer is that these and other apparently basic concepts or institutions reveal themselves from Marx's perspective to be aspects of the system that can only be understood after we have grasped its quintessential nature. Indeed, it will be Marx's purpose to enable us to see *through* the false simplicity by which business enterprise or the market mechanism or the larger structure of the system are ordinarily represented as the elemental building blocks of capitalism. And for this purpose, the "ordinary" commodity offers a special point of entry, just as daily speech or nightly dreams serve as portals through which the psychoanalyst can enter the hidden domain of the unconscious. For Marx, the commodity is the simplest appearance through which we can pass to discover the essence of the system.

The essence is contained in an aspect of the commodity familiar to economics since Aristotle. It is the double nature of a commodity. Commodities are objects that embody usefulness or pleasures for mankind—*use-values* as Marx called them, following the lead of the classical economists. But commodities also embody *exchange value,* the capacity to command other objects or money in the transactions of daily life.

Again since Aristotle, economists have been struck by, and have sought to explain, the relation

96

between these two attributes of a commodity. "The things which have the greatest value in use have frequently little or no value in exchange," writes Adam Smith; "and on the contrary, those which have the greatest value in exchange have frequently little or no value in use. Nothing is more useful than water: but it will purchase scarce any thing. . . . A diamond, on the contrary, has scarce any value in use; but a very great quantity of other goods may frequently be had in exchange for it."[3]

Marx had relatively little to say at first about use-values as a key to capitalist reality. Commodities are useful, he notes, insofar as they combine two elements—matter and labor. "If we take away the useful labour expended on them," he writes, "a material substratum is always left, which is furnished by Nature without the help of man. . . . We see, then, that labour is not the only source of material wealth, of use-values produced by labour. As William Petty says, labour is the father of material wealth, the earth is its mother."[4]

It is not, however, because of its use-values that Marx chooses the commodity as his point of entry into capitalism. The socioanalytic question is raised by the exchange values that commodities "possess." For this attribute of commodities does not reside in them in the way that use-values do—because the labors of men or the properties of the earth are physically incorporated into a bolt of cloth or a sack of grain to give them their

---

[3]*Wealth of Nations*, p. 28. For Aristotle, see *The Nichomachean Ethics*. Book V.

[4]*Capital*, I, p. 134.

capacities to serve their users. Rather, the exchange values possessed by commodities are put there by society. For commodities in society do not exchange *in differing ratios,* as would likely be the case if individual hunters bartered their deer against the salmon caught by individual fishermen. What we find, instead, is that society manages to establish ratios that determine, for all its members, the terms on which deer can be exchanged for salmon (or to generalize the transaction, for money). Thus we learn from the newspaper or from visiting stores that a pound of venison sells for two dollars and a pound of salmon for four dollars, so that a common exchange ratio of 1:2 has taken the place of the innumerable ratios that might have prevailed had individual hunters exchanged their products with individual fishermen. The puzzle of exchange value is how this social determination is made and what it represents.

Here we begin to pry open the commodity. What we find at first, however, is something already discovered and explored by the classical economists. For Marx is only following in the footsteps of Ricardo (and along the broad trail blazed by Smith) when he asserts that the regulating principle by which society establishes its common ratio of exchange is the quantity of labor that is embodied in each commodity, including the labor stored up in the tools or machinery used in its production. Marx would therefore have concurred entirely with Richardo when the latter wrote:

Suppose that in the early stages of society, the bows and arrows of the hunter were of equal value, and of equal

98

durability, with the canoes and implements of the fisherman, both being the produce of the same quantity of labour. Under such circumstances the value of the deer, the produce of the hunter's day's labour, would be exactly equal to the value of the fish, the produce of the fisherman's day's labour.[5]

This assertion that labor is the regulator of exchange values, or prices, is commonly thought to be "the labor theory of value" on which the Marxian analysis of capitalism is conceptually based. But the determination of exchange ratios is by no means the most important consequence for Marx of his analysis of value. On the contrary, what fascinates Marx—and what he chides the classical economists for having failed to note—is the existence of a fundamental question whose answer has already determined that quantities of labor will be the regulators of exchange relationships. *This unexamined question is how we are able to use labor as a means for establishing ratios of exchange.*

For there is nothing in the concrete reality of labor that qualifies it to be a common denominator of "value" within commodities. On the contrary, labor as we see it in life consists of actions as different and as uncomparable as the traditional apples and oranges. The labor that is required to catch a salmon is altogether different from, and unusable for, that needed to capture a deer. Therefore if labor is to become a means of comparing or measuring the values of commodities, the individualized and differentiated activities of hunters and fishermen, farmers and factory workers, must be

[5]Piero Sraffa, ed., *The Works and Correspondence of David Ricardo*, Vol. I, (Cambridge: Cambridge University Press, 1951), p. 26.

reduced to a common kind, as undifferentiated and quantifiable as grain or coal.

Here is where Marx's analysis begins to show its power. For his argument reveals that it requires a particular set of historic circumstances to bring about such a peculiarly "abstract" kind of labor. This particular set of circumstances is, of course, the mode of production called capitalism. Capitalism is a socioeconomic system built on profit gained from production, not from plunder, sharp trading with foreigners, or feudal exactions. It therefore organizes its productive mechanism in such a way as to reduce the costs of production to a minimum. In turn, as Adam Smith was the first to point out, this impels capitalist manufacturers to seek what Smith called a "division of labour"—a method of reducing individuated and differentiated work to routine and regular motions. Thus the profit drive itself creates powerful forces to homogenize labor and to simplify its form.

Not less important, the capitalist mode of production creates a market for labor, rather than a traditional man-master relationship. The prehistory of capitalism, Marx shows, is characterized by a violent separation of peasants and artisans from direct access to, or ownership of, the means of production. Peasants are separated from their lands by the enclosure movement that gives rise to commercial agriculture; artisans are driven from their crafts by the superior efficiency of nascent merchant-capitalist operations.[6]

[6]Among many accounts of this process, let me mention Karl Polanyi, *The Great Transformation* (Boston: Beacon Press, 1957); Maurice Dobb, *Studies in the*

Thus a market for homogenized labor arises because dispossessed peasants and artisans are forced to offer their labor power in the form needed by the social class that now owns the farms and manufacturing establishments. Labor becomes ever simpler as a consequence of the division of tasks; and the labor force becomes the provider of this homogenized labor power because it has no other way of securing a livelihood. In this way the rise of capitalism brings into being a new form of labor which is indeed capable of being bought and sold like coal or grain, a homogeneous commodity called *labor power* created out of the original heterogeneous labors of precapitalist modes.

In this way Marx's socioanalysis reveals that the classical assumption of a common kind of labor within all commodities poses the question for, not the answer to, the problem of value. The labor theory of value in Marx's hands is therefore not merely a key to exchange ratios. Much more important, it is the key to the historic past of capitalism, the clue to the existence of social relationships essential for, but now half-concealed from, capitalist society. What appears to naive eyes as the eternal reality of work, becomes from a Marxist perspective the specific form of work required by the capitalist process. What appears as the eternal personage of the Worker becomes the unique status and discipline of the working person under the duress of capitalist institutions. And what was formerly only a simple unit of wealth called a commodity now appears, in Marx's words, as a "social hieroglyphic."[7]

(2)

The decipherment of the social hieroglyphic of the commodity thus alerts us in the first instance to an important fact: a commodity is not just a thing, but also a container of invisible social relationships. It is this twofold nature of the commodity that mystifies our perception of capitalist realities.

Marx calls this mystification *the fetishism of commodities*. By this he means that the exchangeability of commodities appears to result from their physical properties, not from the hidden social relationships that, by filling them with abstract labor, endow them with their attributes of exchange value. Thus, as Marx writes, a "definite social relation between men themselves . . .

---

[7]*Capital*, I, p. 167. There are numerous problems associated with the labor theory of value that cannot be discussed here. Some of them—for example, the problem of deriving "abstract" labor from the concrete labors of men and women, or the task of reducing complex labor to simple labor—involve difficult, even recondite considerations. The labor theory possesses, however, one advantage of immense importance: it gives meaning to the measurement of aggregate production. Conventional neo-classical theory, which eschews a labor theory, is content to depict aggregate production (such as gross national product) as a sum of priced objects, and does not inquire into any real common denominator of that sum. In fact, each object in the collection is regarded by conventional economics as reflecting in its prices the interplay of the marginal utilities that it affords and the marginal disutilities that it requires for its creation. The idea of gross national product is therefore a summation of individuals' utilities and disutilities.

But such a concept is totally at odds with the conventional economists' premise of the individuality of economic agents. Utilities and disutilities are held to be entirely private states of mind, with no public counterpart to "abstract labor." It is therefore as meaningless to add my utilities and yours as to add my hearing and yours. *This means, however, that there is no objective sense in the assertion that one gross national product is larger than another!* The labor theory avoids this impasse by the assumption that abstract labor allows two disparate collections of objects to be "weighed" to determine which is larger.

assumes . . . the fantastic form of a relation between things.''[8]

There are few insights in all of Marx's writings as striking as the fetishism of commodities—indeed, few in all of social science. The perception that commodities possess the property of exchange value because they are the repositories of an abstract form of labor; that this abstract labor testifies to the social and technical relationships of a specific mode of production; and *that a commodity is therefore the carrier and the encapsulation of the social history of capitalism*—all this comes as a stunning realization.

The realization has many applications, not least the light it throws on our conventional depiction of how wealth arises under capitalism. Economists from early days have taught us that wealth is the result of land, labor, and capital bestowing their respective contributions to the production of useful things. But the land and capital of which economists speak refer only to the thinglike aspects of resources and artifacts, which do indeed always enter into commodities to help endow them with their use-values. Land and capital, however, like labor, are also social relationships—namely, the right accorded to the owners of land and capital to exert a claim on production on behalf of the contribution to output made by ''their'' resources or capital goods. The confusion of this social right with the physical reality of productivity is a central and enduring part of the fetishism that obscures the workings of capitalism. It is be-

[8]Ibid., p. 165.

cause of this confusion that even the most sophisticated economists speak of "land" as if the soil itself, and not the landlord, were being remunerated for its assistance to output, or as if the rewards "due" to capital were paid directly to a machine and not to its owner. Thus capitalism becomes, as Marx describes it, "an enchanted topsy-turvy world, in which Monsieur le Capital and Madame la Terre do their ghost walking as social characters and at the same time as mere things."[9]

Were the hypnosis cast by the fetishism of commodities not so powerful, economics, which scrutinizes the mechanisms and institutions of capitalism, would not be the darling social science of bourgeois culture. The examination of any wealth-gathering system is always potentially dangerous for its ruling classes, whose disproportionate claims on the material output of society must then be explained, whether by an indifferent acquiescence in plunder and exploitation, or by recourse to religious or traditional rationales.[10]

But under the capitalist order, a similar transfer of wealth from those who produce it to those who play little or no direct role in the production of wealth can be subjected, without any qualms, to the most precise "scientific" inquiry. Once land and capital, like labor, have been sanctified into things (a Holy Trinity, Marx called them), all subversive interpretations disappear.

---

[9]*Capital*, III, p. 830.

[10]Thus Aristotle writes, "From the hour of their birth, some are marked out for subjection, some for command" (*Politics*, Book I); or Raymond de Lull, "It is seemly . . . that the knight, who rides and does a lord's work, should get his wealth from the things on which his men spend much toil and fatigue." *Book of the Order of Chivalry*, cited in *Cambridge Economic History*, I, p. 277.

Land, labor, and capital then appear only as things that "cooperate" to create social wealth, each contributing its measurable share, for which each is properly rewarded. The antagonisms and conflicts apparent in the view of these same things as social relationships, in which some classes work and others exert claims of ownership, is effectively screened from view. The Marxian identification of the fetishistic element within the humble commodity is therefore shocking. Each commodity becomes in miniature a congelation of forces locked in combat, not in cooperation. No conventional explanation of the world of commodities can ever again be accepted at face value. In this way, Marx's dissection of the commodity gives us a truly socioanalytic insight into the system.

(3)

So far we have concentrated mainly on the peculiar nature of the labor that endows commodities under capitalism with exchange value. Now we must examine more closely Marx's analysis of the commodity labor power itself. Like all commodities it has a double aspect—usefulness and exchangeability. But Marx has discovered a special attribute of labor power that makes it unlike any other commodity. It is that the act of consuming its use-values yields a "surplus." If bread were labor power, so to speak, we would become rich by eating.

This special attribute of labor power comes about because its use-value lies in the products that are produced *for the capitalist* by the working man or woman during the period of time that he or she labors. One of the conditions of selling labor power as a commodity is that the working person abandons any claim to the product he or she creates. As John Locke could write, without sensing any inconsistency, "the grass my horse has bit, the turfs *my servant* has cut, and the ore I have digged . . . become *my* property without the assignation or consent of anybody."[11] That is why the cars coming off an assembly line, like the turfs that Locke's servant has cut, do not belong to the workers or even to the management, but to the company whose "servants" both workers and management are.

But labor power offered on the market as a commodity, Marx pointed out, also has an exchange value. Like all commodities, that value consists of the labor that has gone into its creation. The labor that goes into the creation of "labor power" is the living labor of the present and the stored-up labor of the past required to "make" the labor power offered on the market. To put it differently, the value of labor power is the wages needed to sustain a worker in his conventional standard of living. This conventional standard need not be a bare minimum. Marx, along with Smith and Ricardo, recognized that "subsistence" was a sociological, not a biological, norm; and that the subsistence required by the labor force would increase as the productive capabilities of society grew.

Nonetheless, in his separation of labor into two constituents—a use-value for the capitalist, determined

[11]My italics. John Locke, *Second Treatise on Government* (Indianapolis: Bobbs-Merrill, 1952, 1975), p. 18.

by the eventual exchange value of the products that labor would create, and an exchange value for the laboring power of the worker, determined by the subsistence wage required by the laborer—Marx discovered what he believed to be the innermost secret of capitalism. The secret is that profit is won not as a result of sharp dealing in the commodity market, but as a normal part of the production process—not in exchange but prior to exchange, in production itself. The source of profit lies in the appropriation by the capitalist of the *surplus value*, or the difference between the value of labor power sold as a commodity by the working class, and the value of the product of that labor power, which accrues to the capitalist at the end of the production process.

The theory of surplus value is central to Marx's socioanalysis and we must take a moment to subject it to critical inquiry. At the core of the idea is the difference between labor and labor power. Labor power is the *capacity for work* that an employer buys when he hires a worker for a day or a week. Labor, on the other hand, is the *actual expenditure of human energy and intelligence* that becomes embodied in the commodities that laborers create. Marx's theory of surplus value asserts that there must be a systematic difference between the two—that one must always be able to buy the capacity for work for less than the value that will be created when that capacity is put to use and commodities are produced. Indeed, it is only because this difference exists that capital itself can be brought into being.

The idea has a prima-facie plausibility in the historic setting in which Marx conceived it, a setting unforgettably portrayed in the ferocious chapter of *Capital* on "The Working Day." As we read the accounts of English factory labor employed for twelve- and fourteen-hour days and paid a near starvation wage, the existence of surplus value seems as undeniable as the naked extraction of a surplus from slave labor. In fact, however, there is no proof that surplus value existed even under these conditions. If wages were low, so was productivity. Competition among employers was fierce, and profits in many sweated trades may have been very low or even nil. Marx's depiction of surplus value carries the conviction of his outraged sense of justice, but even he did not claim to have "proved" its presence by a resort to empirical evidence.

In fact, his intent was not to show its presence by measurement, but by argument. Marx's theory is not one of "unfairness," but of systemic tendencies that will generate surplus value even in situations where there is a formal "equality" of bargaining power, where worker and capitalist meet one another as free agents to enter into wage agreements, and where workers are paid the *full value* of their labor power. For it is his contention that even in such a setting—"the very Eden of the innate rights of man," as he called it[12]—the value of labor power will always be less than the value a capitalist will receive from the commodities that this labor power will produce.

This leads to a very important consequence. If

[12]*Capital,* I, p. 180.

there is surplus value available from hiring labor, one would think that employers would hire more labor to enlarge the base from which they can draw profits. Thus the demand for labor would increase, and wages would rise. Moreover, wages would continue to increase as capitalists continued to compete for access to labor power, until there was no more surplus value to be had—that is, until wages were so high that they left no quantum of unpaid labor within the capitalist's commodities.

To forestall that outcome, the bargaining situation itself, for all its seeming freedom and equality, must be tilted in favor of the capitalist. Marx identifies two such biases, both of which had actually been anticipated by Smith. The first was the weak bargaining power of labor—the consequence of its inability to subsist very long if it held back its labor. "The workman may be as necessary to his master as his master is to him," wrote Adam Smith, "but the need is not so immediate."[13] Marx relies on this inherent inequality in his assumption that workers have nothing to sell but their labor power, and that capitalists have the bulk of society's wealth at their command. Thus workers cannot mount a strike effective enough to secure the payment of wages equal to the value of their output.

The second surplus-value protecting element is a "mechanism" that will prevent wages from rising under the stimulus of competition. Again Smith (and Ricardo) preceded Marx. They believed that the effect

[13]*Wealth of Nations*, p. 66.

of a generalized increase in the demand for labor would be a stimulus to population growth, as the labor force used its increased earnings to produce or rear more children to working age (Smith estimated child mortality at about fifty percent). Marx has no dealings with such population reflexes. But his scheme also relieves the squeeze on surplus value by matching an increase in the demand for labor with an increase in its supply. This comes about because Marx sees the pressure of competition inducing employers to introduce cost-cutting, labor-saving machinery. Technological unemployment thereby creates a "relative overpopulation" that plays the same role as the absolute rise in population proposed by the classical economists.

Thus, in Marx's view, the weak bargaining position of labor and the pressure of unemployment both operate systematically to maintain the value of the commodity labor power below the level to which it would otherwise be forced by the competitive bidding of capitalists. Note that these depressant forces do not affect any other commodity; for instance, the machines that capitalists produce and sell to one another. If there is a "surplus" to be gained from the use of a machine, capitalists will bid for it until its price rises to the full value that the machine embodies. Therefore, there can be no permanent layer of surplus available from machines comparable to that which is maintained within labor power. Labor alone contains a potentially available source of profit. This conclusion, as we shall see, has great significance for the fate of the system.

Before we proceed to that topic, however, there is a question that requires further exploration. It is whether the theory of surplus value is still relevant in the changed institutional and dynamic conditions of modern capitalism. Does an imbalance in bargaining strength and an undertow of technological unemployment still bring about a permanent differential between the price of labor power—the wages paid to labor—and the value of the labor that is obtained for the payment of these wages?

Curiously, the matter cannot be settled by direct inspection. Value is an abstract concept, like energy in physics. We do not know, and have no way of measuring, how much "abstract labor" may be embodied in a General Motors car, or whether there is a difference between the labor power for which General Motors pays its wages and the labor it receives in exchange. Between the abstract world of values and the concrete world of prices and wages lies the push and pull of the marketplace. Values, in Marx's scheme, reflect only the outpouring of labor energies, reduced to some common denominator. Prices reflect actual costs, and the ebb and flow of supply and demand. These prices need not—and as Marx pointed out *cannot*—correspond precisely to values. Thus the concrete sum we call "profit" is not the same as the abstract sum of surplus value.[14]

[14]Here lies the source of the famous, and still controversial, "transformation problem." Marx assumes that competition creates a uniform rate of surplus value—that employers in all fields extract the same proportion of surplus value from their workers. He also assumes, as do all economists, that competition brings about a more or less uniform rate of profit that employers earn on their total capital. It is

Therefore the relevance of the theory of surplus value must be judged by different criteria. Specifically, we must ask whether the presence of differential class bargaining power, or of technological unemployment, still act to depress wages—the value of labor power—below the value that labor power creates.

Even this is a question difficult to answer with certitude. Insofar as the bargaining position of labor is concerned, undoubtedly the balance has greatly changed since Marx's time. In some industries—those employing farm workers, for example—the superior bargaining strength of the employer is still patently in evidence. In others, such as the garment industry, the preponderance of power may now have swung to labor's side, which often holds the threat of bankruptcy over its employers' heads. In big businesses, the strength of corporations and unions is more evenly matched than in the past.

Against this institutional redress of bargaining power, however, must be placed the deliberate efforts of all capitalist governments to prevent labor's strength from "getting out of hand"—that is, from raising wages until profits are squeezed out. In many modern capitalisms, for example, we find the importation of

---

apparent, however, that employers do not combine labor and capital (machinery or other nonliving means of production) in the same ratios in all fields. Yet, because Marx assumes that profits arise only from labor, not machinery, the question then arises as to how a common rate of profit can emerge from production processes with unequal labor/capital ratios. The answer is that the market must cause the prices of production to diverge systematically from their values, in order to redistribute surplus values equally in all lines of business. Marx does not demonstrate this process very satisfactorily, and it has engaged the attention of Marxist (and non-Marxist) economists ever since. For a recent review of the problem, see *Journal of Economic Literature*, January 1971, and March 1972 and 1973.

cheap labor from low-wage nations, such as Italy, Greece, Yugoslavia, Turkey, or Portugal. This is a policy that is explained by the importing governments as being necessary in order to get personnel to perform work that domestic workers will no longer do. What is meant, in fact, is that domestic workers will not do the work except at wages that cannot be tolerated, *because they would make profits impossible.*

Unemployment also continues to act as a pressure against wage increases. Whether this unemployment is primarily generated by technological displacement, or by the recurrent crises also envisaged by Marx, is difficult to say, but it hardly matters. For in their place we find capitalist governments deliberately ''trading off'' unemployment against inflation—which is to say, *creating* unemployment in order to hold down wage increases, and thereby to restrain inflation.

Therefore I think it is reasonable to assume that labor power sells for less than it would in the absence of pressures produced directly or indirectly by capital itself. To put it differently, wages would rise if labor were stronger, and labor *would* be stronger if its bargaining position were not undermined by economic processes and political policies rooted in the capitalist system. Although this does not ''prove'' the existence of surplus value (which in any event can never be empirically demonstrated), it is certainly a necessary condition if surplus value is still to exist. *This does not mean, however, that all bookkeeping profit derives from surplus value.* Marx himself recognized the possibility that individual capitalists could increase their profits through monopolistic market power, or by technological advantages, or by "unequal exchanges" abroad. He might concede that these are greater sources of profits for large-scale business than in his day; and that some of the forces against wage increases—notably, the worker's lack of bargaining power—had been considerably alleviated by the formation of powerful unions and welfare-support systems.[15]

The existence of surplus value therefore remains an unprovable proposition exactly as it was in Marx's time. It is a heuristic rather than an operational concept. Its importance lies in its identification of the class struggle and the fetishism of commodities as the two essential elements in producing and rationalizing the surplus that is produced by one class and appropriated by another.

As such, the theory of surplus value provides an explanation for a problem that has always been the Achilles' heel of economics, namely, the source of profits. Unwilling to attribute profits to the transfer of wealth from one class to another, bourgeois economists have struggled in vain to explain profits, not as a transient monopoly return or an evanescent technological advantage, but as a *persistent, central feature of the system of capitalism.*

To a limited extent Adam Smith acknowledged the source of all profits in a "deduction" from the reward to labor, and to a bolder, but still incomplete degree,

---

[15]For a recent effort to reconcile the theory of surplus value with corporate profits, see Ernest Mandel, *Late Capitalism,* (London: New Left Books, 1975), Chapter 3. For the international transfer of surplus, see Arrghiri Emmanuel, *Unequal Exchange* (New York: Monthly Review Press, 1972).

Ricardo did the same. Thereafter all efforts to explain profits disappeared before the fetishism that attributed rent to the productivity of the "land," and interest or profits to that of "capital." Marx's contribution was not only to remove the disguise that allowed "land" and "capital" to appear as things, rather than social relations, but also to explain how the forces generated by the capitalist mode could systematically depress the values of labor power below the value that it bequeathed to commodities. The purpose of the theory of surplus value is therefore to explain what is otherwise inexplicable: the presence of an enduring, although ever-threatened, surplus within the capitalist mode of production. As such, it remains an essential part of Marx's socioanalysis, without which we cannot penetrate to the core of the capitalist system.[16]

(4)

The exploration of surplus value has taken us deep into the interior of capitalism. But we have not yet

[16]An often heard criticism is that the validity of the labor theory of value is vitiated by the extraordinary power of modern-day technology. This is another example of the fetishism of commodities, leading us to confuse machinery as a source of use-value with its role as a source of exchange value. Marx himself anticipated this objection in a remarkable passage in the *Grundrisse:*

[T]o the degree that large industry develops, the creation of real wealth comes to depend less on labour time and on the amount of labour employed, than on the power of the agencies set in motion during labour time, whose 'powerful effectiveness' . . . depends . . . on the general state of science and on the progress of technology. . . . Labour no longer appears so much to be included within the production process; rather, the human being comes to relate more as watchman and regulator to the production process itself.

Yet, Marx goes on to say, in words that reveal the fetishism at work:

Nature builds no machines, no locomotives, railways, electric telegraphs, self-acting mules, etc. These are products of human industry. . . . They are *organs of the human brain, created by the human hand;* the power of knowledge, objectified.

(*Grundrisse*, pp. 704–706. Marx's italics.)

encountered the very identificatory element of the system, capital itself.

"Capital," according to Marx, "is self-expanding value."[17] What meaning can these words have? We usually conceive capital as an assemblage of things, as the physical embodiment of expended labor. As such, capital is an inanimate object—dead labor, Marx calls it—and cannot possess will and purpose. What does it mean, then, to speak of capital as "self-expanding value"?

The answer, of course, recalls Marx's insistence on the social relations expressed within the commodity. Capital is far more than an assemblage of equipment. The labor of the past, now incorporated in a machine, does not work with the living labor of the present as its servant, as a gift of the past to be put to whatever use best suits its beneficiaries in the present. Rather, dead labor—machinery—faces living labor as its master. Living labor must adapt its motions to the requirements of its dead counterpart, and those requirements were not built into the machine to enhance the work experience of living labor, but to maximize the possibility of using it to create as much surplus value, the source of new capital, as possible.

Everyone knows that machinery is not created to maximize the sheer pleasures of work, but to maximize output. It may be objected that this is an engineering criterion of efficiency, not a capitalist one. But the definition of "efficiency" is one that emphasizes the greatest possible physical output at the lowest possible

[17]*Capital*, II, p. 105.

economic cost. In capitalism, considerations that lie outside this calculus—for example, the pacing of work to interest the operator, or the design of work to employ the operator's intelligence—are simply irrelevant, or counterproductive. Such considerations are admitted only to the extent that they do not interfere with, or possibly improve, the performance of *profitable* work.[18]

Thus capital exists within the capitalist mode of production as a social relation of domination, an expression of the hierarchy of class structure that can be found in all societies. What is overt in other societies, however, is disguised in capitalism. In the latter, capital seems to exist as a vast lever at the disposal of mankind, not as a disciplinary device over mankind. So it is that we "obey" the rhythms of the machine and dance to the tune of money, hardly aware that we are following the dictates of a social, not a natural, imperative.

This insight clarifies an important problem. It pinpoints the origin of that apparently irresistible urge to expand that endows capitalism with its restless, demonic character, its self-imposed sentence of interminable profit-seeking. The concept of capital as a social relation expressing class domination allows us to see that the "self-expanding" drive is much more than greed. It is the expression of the class struggle, in which the dominant class seeks to maintain its position of superiority. It maintains that superiority by constantly

[18]For a brilliant and searching description of the subordination of the work process to the dictates of capitalist criteria, see Harry Braverman, *Labor and Monopoly Capital* (New York: Monthly Review Press, 1974).

renewing and expanding its accumulation of capital—
the very enforcement agency of its power over labor.

Capital expands because the social relation of
domination cannot be a passive one. But there is also a
second compelling force. Capitalism is controlled by
competitive market relationships, not only in its contractual arrangements between labor and capital, but
also among capitalists themselves. Here competition is
the dominant force exerted by the marketplace, a competition that itself originates in the expansive, accumulative drives of individual "capitals," or enterprises. Competition manifests itself in the continuous
threat that each capital poses to every other, a threat that
can only be effectively countered if each enterprise
itself adopts an aggressive, expansive strategy. Thus the
sheer necessity for self-preservation also forces
capitalists to seek to expand. "Accumulate, accumulate! That is Moses and the prophets," writes Marx.[19]

From the necessity of the accumulative drive
comes that celebration of acquisitiveness that is so much
a part of capitalist culture. "An augmentation of fortune
is the means by which the greater part of men propose
and wish to better their condition," writes Adam Smith;
and the wish to better our condition, he states, "comes
with us from the womb, and never leaves us till we go
into the grave."[20] Or as Marx comments, "This boundless drive for enrichment, this passionate chase after
value, is common to the capitalist and the miser, but
while the miser is merely a capitalist gone mad, the
capitalist is a rational miser."[21]

[19]*Capital*, I, p. 752.
[20]*Wealth of Nations*, pp. 324.
[21]*Capital*, I, 254.

In our next section we shall investigate the laws of motion to which this expansive drive gives rise. Before doing so, we should note a crucially important result of that profit-seeking impulse. It is that the insatiable acquisitiveness imparted to capital in general, and to individual capitals in particular, produce a regularity of direction for the activities of the system. When Marx speaks of the laws of motion of capitalism, he is referring—as did Smith and Ricardo before him and almost all economists after him—to the presence within capitalism of behavior patterns that enable an observer to foresee the path of the social mechanism.

Therefore capitalism obeys laws of motion that differentiate it from other socioeconomic formations. The fates of Asiatic despotisms or of city-states or ancient empires did not at the time, and do not retrospectively, appear to be preordained by their immanent behavioral propensities. It is the peculiar nature of capitalism alone that its fate seems to be the inevitable consequence of the conflicting elements within it. This extraordinary property of capitalism led the eighteenth-century philosophe, the Abbé Mably, to muse, "Is society, then, a branch of physics?" This same property allows Marx, as Smith and Ricardo before him, to envisage society as a *system in motion* whose trajectory and destination can be deduced from its expansive tendencies and its channeling institutions.

(5)

Thus we reach the laws of motion of the system. Here we enter upon a theoretical territory that is not only vast, but that has been greatly enlarged since Marx's time as the explanations of capitalism have been revised to fit developments unforeseen or only dimly perceived by Marx himself.[22] I shall make very little effort to explore these modernizations of Marx's model—the essential elements of nearly all of them lie in a few central conceptions that we have already discovered. The great bulk of writing on capitalism after Marx, in other words, constitutes an elaboration and extension of the laws of motion already specified in *Capital* itself.

It will help organize our task if we consider these laws under two rubrics. One of them concerns the trajectory of the system as a whole—a trajectory that we know points in the direction of the ultimate breakdown of capitalism and its supersession by socialism. But a second category of the laws of motion is no less important, although perhaps less dramatic. It consists of the "micro"-movements, the changes in texture and configuration, that are also produced by the larger "macro"-movements of the system. As we shall see, these intrasystemic movements are indispensable for the realization of the larger movements of the system as a whole.

Let us begin with the mise-en-scène for the larger drama. A competitive market system brings together workers and capitalists, the latter offering employment to the former, the former offering their

[22]A complete citation is not possible here. Merely to indicate some facets of the literature, let me mention the work of Rosa Luxemburg, Lenin, and a vast number of writers on the subject of imperialism and the internationalization of capital; the development of a huge sociological literature around the problems of class and ideology, of which the work of Lukács and of the Frankfurt School are important exemplars; and the extension of "classical" Marxism into a theory of monopoly capitalism, an effort that begins with Hilferding and that has produced an enormous body of economic analysis.

working abilities to the latter. Through the alchemy of the labor process, which we have examined, surplus value accrues to the capitalist; from surplus value emerge its money counterparts—profits, interest, and rent.

What interests us now is the contradiction into which this initial mise-en-scène forces the system. We have already identified its elements. An inherent movement toward expansion impels all capitalists to seek an augmentation of their capitals. This system-wide impetus leads to an increased demand for labor. Wages rise; profits are accordingly reduced. Capitalists thereupon attempt to maintain their profits in the only way open to them, by substituting machinery for labor in an effort to cut costs and undersell competitors.

The realism of this description of business expansion is evident. But what Marx now reveals is the *contradictory* nature of the capitalists' response—a response at once necessary for their self-protection and instrumental in their self-destruction. For the introduction of machinery, however successful for the pioneering capitalist, brings adverse results as it is generalized across the system. The reason is that the replacement of living labor by dead labor—the replacement of a work force by machinery—narrows the base from which surplus value can be drawn. Machinery or other goods can never be a source of surplus value, since, as we have seen, the competitive bidding process will eliminate any difference between the price of such machinery or goods and their monetary worth for the capitalist who buys them. Therefore, as labor is displaced by machinery, the ability of a given sum of capital to yield surplus value must fall. *Thus the contradiction of the expansion process is that it leads in the direction of a falling rate of profit,* or as Marx carefully phrased it in Volume III of *Capital,* a "law of the tendency of the rate of profit to fall."

Marx's phraseology—the *tendency*—is not merely a circumlocution. It is meant to emphasize that the falling rate of profit emerges from conflicting forces whose outcome cannot be mechanically predicted. Ricardo believed that the rate of profit would fall because the extension of agriculture to less productive lands would exert an inescapable force of nature against the economic product available as profit. Marx believed it would fall only as the consequence of a crosscurrent of *social* forces. He lists, in fact, five such principal counteracting social forces that may reverse the downward pressure on profits: increasing the intensity of exploitation (for example, running an assembly line faster); depressing wages below the value of labor power (sweating labor, when conditions permit); taking advantage of business crises to buy machinery or raw materials below their true values; using unemployed labor to produce new types of commodities; and garnering surplus value abroad through foreign trade.

These counteracting influences make it impossible to foretell that the rate of profit will decline at a given rate or within a fixed period of time. All that Marx expects is that profit rates will always be subject to erosion as mechanization steadily displaces the source from which all profits must ultimately arise. Meanwhile, however, this falling tendency is subjected to fluctuations, both upwards and downwards, by a succession of capitalist "crises" that are also an integral part of the expansionary process. For as the system drives ahead in its tension-ridden, uncoordinated way, it typically veers toward one or another of two poles. On the one hand, capital accumulation may proceed too rapidly, giving rise to a general crisis of "overinvestment," with symptoms of excessive plant expansion, inflated wage and other costs, and overstrained credit facilities; or the expansionary thrust may veer in the opposite direction, with lagging sales and disappointing business results stemming from "underconsumption"—a failure of mass buying power to sustain the volume of output.

Thus the larger laws of motion do not dictate, in themselves, a system marching in a straight path to its doom. Rather, what we have from the major internal contradiction of the process—the self-defeating substitution of machinery for labor—is a system under endemic stress, always subject to a downward tendency of profits, but again and again rescued by counteracting forces whose influence can, in the short run, easily outpull the slow undertow of the mechanization process.

If anything summarizes this flux of contrary forces, it is Marx's word *anarchy*, a term he uses to describe the contradictions inherent in the idea of capital itself. "The real barrier to capitalist production," he writes, "is *capital itself*."[23] By this Marx calls atten-

---

[23]Marx's italics. *Capital*, III, p. 250.

tion to the irreconcilable conflict between the forces of production that are ever more technically interconnected, scientifically complex, and rationally unified, and the relations of production that remain stubbornly individualist, competitive, and antagonistic. The doom of capitalism is that it creates technical structures of production that exceed its institutions of social control.

Yet the pushes and pulls of the business cycle, or the counteracting tendencies working against the erosion of surplus value, would not in themselves necessarily bring the system to a point at which this final contradiction proved insuperable. What gives a cumulative impetus to the flux of events is something we have not yet considered—the effects of the micromovements of the system.

By far the most important of these effects is the systematic change in the size and unification of command of the typical capitalist enterprise. Marx calls this process the *concentration* and *centralization* of capital. It is the process by which giant companies become the typical operational units of mature capitalism, as successful businesses generate additional capital from their own sales and as they acquire the assets of weaker competitors during periods of crisis.

Thus the succession of crises brings about a steady change in the texture of the economic system. Concentration and centralization alter the universe of atomistic capitals into one of macromolecular capitals. With this change comes an intensification of the effects of crisis, for large enterprises create major wreckage when they go under. The severity of crisis thereby becomes ever more acute.

The succession of worsening crises changes the political scene as well as the economic setting. As the large corporations expand, they winnow the ranks of weaker capitalist elements. "One capitalist always kills many," comments Marx.[24] Thus we find the petty capitalist pushed to the wall and reduced to proletarian—wage-earning—status, just as the independent peasant proprietor and artisan were proletarianized earlier in capitalism's history. The social classes of capitalism are thereby purged of intermediate elements and appear ever more starkly as two opposing camps—the great majority who have no access to livelihood except through the sale of their labor power, and a small class of capitalists who own the great bulk of the means of production. Meanwhile, the confused perceptions of the working class are exposed to repeated hammer blows that gradually forge the metal of a revolutionary consciousness.

In this way, the interior movements of the system impart a trend to its fluctuations, bringing the series of crises toward the climax of a catastrophic final crisis. Marx does not directly describe a specific mechanism of collapse. In consequence, there has been considerable disagreement among his successors as to the timing, and nature, and inevitability of "breakdown." Only once in the 2500-odd pages of *Capital* does he indulge in an apocalyptic vision of the ultimate destination of the system:

[24]Ibid., I, p. 763.

Hand in hand with this . . . expropriation of many capitalists by a few, other developments take place on an ever-expanding scale, such as the growth of the co-operative form of the labour process, the conscious technical application of science, the planned exploitation of the soil, the transformation of the means of labour into forms in which they can be used in common, the economizing of all means of production by their use as the means of production of combined, socialized labour, the entanglement of all peoples in the net of the world market, and, with this, the growth of the international character of the capitalist regime. Along with the constant decrease in the number of capitalist magnates, who usurp and monopolize all the advantages of this process of transformation, the mass of misery, oppression, slavery, degradation and exploitation grows; but with this there also grows the revolt of the working class, a class constantly increasing in numbers, and trained, united and organized by the very mechanism of the capitalist process of production. The monopoly of capital becomes a fetter upon the mode of production which has flourished alongside and under it. The centralization of the means of production and the socialization of labour reach a point at which they become incompatible with their capitalist integument. The integument is burst asunder. The knell of capitalist private property sounds. The expropriators are expropriated.[25]

---

[25]*Capital,* I, p. 929. It might be noted that this exceptional passage is accompanied by an equally exceptional effort to introduce a dialectical note directly into the analysis of economic change. The paragraph that follows the citation above reads:

The capitalist mode of appropriation, which springs from the capitalist mode of production, produces capitalist private property. This is the first negation of individual private property, as founded on the labour of its proprietor. But capitalist production begets, with the inexorability of a natural process, its own negation. This is the negation of the negation. It does not reestablish private property, but it does indeed establish individual property on the basis of the achievements of the capitalist era: namely cooperation and the possession in common of the land and the means of production produced by labour itself.

The attempt to explain the rise of capitalist ownership and its eventual displacement by socialist forms of property by dialectical "laws" is one of the few

(6)

The prospect of collapse brings us to the threshold of the next mode of production, presumably socialism. But before we go on, we should take a critical look at the laws of motion whose general pattern and direction we have sought to describe. For this purpose it might be well to begin with the question of the historical confirmation or disconfirmation of Marx's general system.

One must begin with the clear recognition that the crowning event in the great drama of Marx's thought has not been realized. Not a single proletarian revolution has occurred in any industrialized capitalist nation. Moreover, there is no clear evidence that the system as a whole is now approaching a final "breakdown." For a period during the decade of the 1930s, it seemed as if the scenario of *Capital* was likely to be shortly fulfilled, as capitalism sank into severe depression, and revolutionary working-class movements appeared in Germany, France, and, to a lesser extent, in England. But that moment passed and capitalism emerged from World War II with rediscovered vitality. Economic growth at an unprecedented pace, expansion of capitalism around the world at a headlong rate, evaporation of the revolutionary mood, and the creation of "welfare states" in virtually all capitalist nations seemed to disprove, once and for all, the validity of Marx's laws of motion,

---

times when Marx uses the dialectic not as a means of inquiry but as an explanation of a causal sequence. It is not, I think, a legitimate use. The suggestion that dialectical contradictions arise "with the inexorability of a natural process" reduces dialectics to a truism, or misconceives the problem as I have defined it, which is to locate and identify those processes in society that have the necessary properties of a "contradiction."

and of the elaborations and extensions of those laws among his followers.

Certainly such a resurgence of capitalism was not foreseen by Marx himself, who, though always guarded in his statements, probably did not expect capitalism to last far into the twentieth century. Nor was the renewal of capitalism (or the appearance of revolutionary movements in noncapitalist countries) anticipated by the succession of analysts who followed Marx, most of whom freely predicted the more or less imminent decline of capitalism. Thus, as a large-scale "predictive" model, Marx's scenario must be declared a failure. Moreover, Marxist economics since Marx has also failed in correctly predicting the main trajectory of the system, and has mainly been concerned with explaining events after they have occurred.[26]

[26]Marxist economics shares this fate with conventional economics, and for the same reason. Despite its recourse to the insights or methods of dialectics, Marxian economic analysis, like conventional analysis, depends for its predictive power on its specification of behavior and its accurate description of institutional constraints, even though it derives its views of behavior and institutions in a unique, dialectical manner. Only if Marxian analysis could specify behavior differently from conventional analysis, or if it could identify critical junctures at which behavior would change, or if it had a keener understanding of the nature and effects of institutional constraints, would its predictive power be inherently greater than conventional prediction. In fact, however, Marxian analysis also relies on a simple "maximizing" concept of behavior, has no means of accurately anticipating inflection points, and possesses little if any operational advantage in its institutional grasp. Thus its predictive models, although based on different initial concepts or relationships than conventional models, grind out equally mechanical forecasts.

This does not dispose of the matter, however. Rather, it raises the question as to whether "prediction" is an appropriate or realistic criterion for social analysis. There is growing doubt that social science can ever predict social events with accuracy, in part because it is never possible to eliminate (even in thought) all the "impurities" in the social test tube, and also because behavior becomes intrinsically difficult to specify or predict in the more "permissive" climate of mature capitalism. (See A. Lowe, *On Economic Knowledge*, [New York: Harper and Row, 1965, 1972], Chapter 3.) Instead of prediction, the ability to *control* outcomes may become the test of the "scientific" validity of social theory, with all the dangers of this kind of unity of theory and practice.

But control is often not feasible in history. It is possible, then, that the proper

Yet there is another side to the coin. For a number of the intrasystemic prognoses made by Marx and his successors *have* been vindicated by history. The rise of large-scale industry, the internationalization of capital, the continuous squeeze of technology on employment, the rising "mechanization" of capital, are all laws of motion that have been brilliantly confirmed.

Equally striking has been the centralization of capital inherent in the dynamics of Marx's analysis: the one-hundred largest enterprises in the United States, for example, which collectively possessed no more than a few percent of the nation's business assets in 1870, owned almost fifty percent of all manufacturing assets a century later. No less prescient was the prediction of the rising "proletarianization" of the public, a prognosis that seems at first directly disconfirmed by the growing numbers of "middle-class" citizens within capitalism. But if we define a proletarian, as did Marx, as a worker who has no direct ownership of the means of production, the projected trend is strikingly confirmed. In the 1800s, self-employed farmers and urban artisans comprised about eighty percent of the American population.

---

objectives for social science, Marxist or not, is clarification and understanding, even if these do not lead to hypotheses that can then be falsified by positivist criteria. To be sure, this leaves social science in general, and Marxism in particular, with the necessity to discover some means of distinguishing valid clarifications and understandings from invalid ones. This returns us to the dilemma with which Marxism finds itself vis-à-vis positivism (see Chapter II, p. 50). There is a tendency for Marxists to wish to have their cake and eat it too, pointing in triumph to historical prognostications that have been fulfilled, and excusing those that have not by the arguments I have just raised. There is, perhaps, no escape from this predicament. I do not see how one can avoid some search for a general "vindication" in history, although this is inherently less sharp and decisive than a specific prediction. History is a lengthy process, however, and does not always offer vindications. The test of clarification and understanding may then have no "test" other than argument, weakly supported by reference to events. To warn against this difficulty, I have eschewed the word prediction and used the term "prognosis" instead.

By 1970 only ten percent of all workers were self-employed. The majority worked for capital, selling its labor power and relinquishing any claim over the products or services it created.

Connected with the prognosis of proletarianization are the famous, perhaps infamous, statements about "immiseration," often cited as examples of Marx's failure to foresee the main thrust of capitalism.[27] Insofar as these statements imply a decline in the material conditions of life for the working man, they are of course flatly contradicted by history, at least in the industrialized world. In fact, however, the older Marx of *Capital* does not repeat the "pauperization" arguments of his pamphlet of 1848; and later Marxists, seeking to reconcile a seeming glaring contradiction of text and history, have turned to a second, not illegitimate, interpretation of Marx's meaning. Their view of "immiseration" stresses the stultification of labor under the conditions of extreme division of labor, a view already forcefully advanced by the Scottish historians of the eighteenth century, including not least Adam Smith, who wrote of the workman in industry: "[He] generally becomes as stupid and ignorant as it is

[27]These statements are to be found in the *Manifesto:* "The modern labourer sinks deeper and deeper below the conditions of existence of his own class. He becomes a pauper, and pauperism develops more rapidly than population and wealth. . . ." A different and more cautious formulation is in *Capital* (I, p. 799): ". . . in proportion as capital accumulates, the situation of the labourer, be his payment high or low, must grow worse. . . . Accumulation at one pole is, therefore, at the same time accumulation of misery, the torment of labour, slavery, ignorance, brutalization and moral degradation, at the opposite pole . . ." Surprisingly similar views were held by Adam Smith: "Wherever there is great property, there is great inequality. For one very rich man there must be at least five hundred poor, and the affluence of the few supposes the indigence of the many" (*Wealth of Nations,* p. 670). Also see his remarks on degradation below.

possible for a human creature to become. . . . [T]he nobler parts of the human character may be, in a great measure, obliterated and extinguished in the great body of the people.''[28]

In sum, it is difficult to know how to judge the prognosis of immiseration—a prognosis made only in passing, but certainly of more than passing importance. Factory labor under capitalism does rob labor systematically of its human rhythm and meaning; urban working-class existence, if it does not make men ''torpid'' as Smith suggests, fills them with shallow learning and ''smart'' ways. Yet in the *Manifesto,* Marx himself calls attention to the ''idiocy'' of rural life, and there is no gainsaying that capitalism has greatly alleviated for most workers the grim bleakness of the working-class life for which it was originally responsible. In all likelihood the proletariat of Dickens's or Marx's day was both economically and socially immiserated in comparison with the tenant peasant-farmer class whence it originated (although not in contrast with the Hogarthian underclass that was the product of mercantilism); but the proletariat of modern capitalism in the West has largely escaped from these rigors. The question, then, may be whether immiseration is a phase through which the proletariat will pass. This question may be tested in the backward nations where a new proletariat, largely created by the disruptive entrance of capitalism, has plunged millions into urban factory life that is immiserated by any standard. Whether this new proletariat can

[28]*Wealth of Nations,* pp. 734, 736.

also pass through the gauntlet while remaining within a capitalist socioeconomic framework, is a matter that we will not know for some decades.

Perhaps of greater importance is the verdict of history with regard to Marx's general analytical finding that capitalism is inherently "anarchic." Here again I do not see how the verdict can be other than positive. The history of capitalism has been a chronicle of economic expansion interrupted and accompanied by the kinds of malfunctions that derive precisely from the absence of a mechanism capable of bringing the private aims of capital into harmony with the social needs of the community. The mechanism of the market, with its vaunted allocative effectiveness, has not been sufficient to curb—indeed has been at the root of—such typical capitalist problems as depression, inflation, the uneven distribution of income, the imbalance between public and private provisions, the "externalities" of pollution, and the like. The persistence of these failures provides a massive confirmation of the fundamental logic of the Marxian analysis, in that these anarchic properties of capitalism follow from the deepest social and historical properties of the system, and not from circumstantial accidents.

No aspect of that anarchic charcter is more pronounced in our own day, or is more the object of Marxist description and analysis, than the internationalization of capital. Hinted at by Marx as one of the forces that would counteract the tendency of the falling rate of profit, developed by Lenin into a full-fledged theory of imperialist conquest and by Rosa Luxemburg into a supposed means of rescuing capitalism from its internal contradictions, the internationalization of capital today testifies to the extraordinary power of capital as "self-expanding value"—that is, to the imperious need for economic organizations, built on the purchase of labor power and the sale of commodities, to seek continuous growth.

This thrust to expansion, first expressed in the creation of large domestic companies, extends itself on a global basis as the development of the technology of transportation and communication shrinks the world. As a consequence, capital moves around the planet in startling fashion, transplanting its centers of manufacturing to cheap "backward" areas, treating the entire globe as one unified potential market. The multinational corporation is of course the fullest expression of this thrust.

The anarchic aspects of this movement are so evident as scarcely to require exposition. Technology is introduced into preindustrial areas with no regard for the needs of the population, but only for those of capital. Populations are pressed into new occupations without heed for the effect on their health, economic security, or opportunities for development, but again solely to serve the requirements of expansive capital. Governments are cajoled and pressured to adopt policies, both with respect to "home" and "host" nations, that facilitate the process of internationalization of capital, justified not by any broad consideration of human requirements around the globe, but according to a calculus of "economic efficiency" that is measured almost exclusively by the touchstone of profitability.

Thus the world "develops" or industrializes not according to the exercise of reason or foresight—frail reeds though these may be—but by the dictates of capital as self-expanding value. The consequence is a world continuously in imbalance—monetary imbalance, trade imbalance, resource imbalance, developmental imbalance. And this imbalance will continue—despite the best efforts of governments to patch up or offset its more dangerous manifestations—as long as the economic unfolding of world history is left to the stimulus of private accumulation. That is the true measure of the anarchy of capital today, the most convincing and the most portentous of all the implications of Marx's thought.

Much less reliable has been the Marxian prognosis of a growing political consciousness, a burgeoning proletarian revolutionary spirit. This theme, sounded by Marx, advanced by Lenin, explored by Lukács and others, has least accorded with Marx's underlying convictions and hopes.

On the contrary, owing no doubt to the rising standard of material well-being of the working classes after about 1870, the history of capitalism since the publication of *Capital* has been marked on the whole with a gradual suffusion of bourgeois attitudes into the working class, of a "bourgeoisification" of the proletariat of which Engels had already taken notice in 1858.[29] Thus the crucial "superstructural" element of

[29]For Engels's remark see Hal Draper, *Karl Marx's Theory of Revolution* (New York: Monthly Review Press, 1978) p. 62.

political awareness has not been added to the "base" economic trends. As a result, revolution has failed to materialize. Indeed, the productive successes of capitalism—clearly recognized but yet insufficiently appreciated by Marx—have not only defused the revolutionary temper of the working class, but have nurtured a growth of conservative sentiment that has strongly tied workers in most capitalist nations to the preservation of the existing system.

Much of this change in working-class attitudes has been the consequence of the development of welfare institutions designed to buffer the anarchic tendencies of capitalism and to create a basis for cementing the political loyalties of the "alienated" workers. This growing importance of the welfare state, and the stubbornly held "false consciousness"—that is, the conservative political and social views—of the working class have become central problems for Marxian analysis, beginning with the work of the Frankfurt School in the 1930s and continuing to the present. Indeed, one of the main tendencies in latter-day Marxism has been an effort to rid itself of the conception, inherited from *Anti-Dühring* and from some incautious remarks of Marx, that the state could be dismissed as the "executive committee" of the bourgeoisie, and that political activity (save for the exercise of revolutionary leadership) was a matter of secondary importance in the understanding of capitalism. That earlier dismissive attitude has now given way to one which stresses the inescapable involvement of the state in the maintenance of capitalism as a social order—a task that brings both economic and political or ideological problems in tow.[30]

The political prognosis for capitalism is therefore difficult to establish. Marxist thought has been torn between millennial hopes and bitter despairs. The expected clarification of proletarian attitudes has not taken place. Yet a tension continues to inhabit capitalism as a consequence of the systematic distortion of perceptions inherent in its fetishistic conception of commodity relations. Whether that deception can be indefinitely continued depends on the corrosive penetration of radical ideas, themselves (like Marxism itself) the product of bourgeois culture. In the end, if we are to believe so staunch a defender of capitalist conventions as Joseph Schumpeter, this self-destroying, immanent skepticism of bourgeois thought will have its way, and the sustaining and cohering beliefs of capitalism will lose their self-evident appeal. But that would give capitalism a longer lease on life than expected by Marx, and would not necessarily lead to the same political outcome, even though Schumpeter also believed that "socialism" was the destined next stage of historical evolution.[31]

In the end, then, to sum up this long chapter, for and against. The negative judgments, it must be clear, apply to the reliability of the laws of motion, at least on

[30]Among recent works that develop this theme, see James O'Connor, *The Fiscal Crisis of the State* (New York: St. Martins Press, 1973); Jürgen Habermas, *Legitimization Crisis* (Boston: Beacon Press, 1973); Nicos Poulantzas, *Political Power and Social Classes* (New York: Schocken Books, 1978).

[31]Joseph A. Schumpeter, *Capitalism, Socialism and Democracy* (New York: Harper and Row, 1947), Chapters V, XIV.

the grand historical scale. Anarchic disruptions do not imply necessary collapse, for the recovery powers and inherent vitality of capital are still vast. Political confusion and lack of revolutionary will may continue for a very long period, even if the maintenance of a capitalist ideology must struggle against the slowly growing force of a radical, critical perspective.

Marx's analysis of the laws of motion of capitalism points in the direction of change on a world-shaking scale. Yet it gives little clue as to the immediate sequence of historical events which, if the past is any guide, will continue to take Marxists and non-Marxists alike by surprise. It is a sobering counterpoint to those who would like to find a guide to the future in Marx's laws of motion, that the three most likely causes for seismic disturbance in the next century—population pressure, nuclear armaments, and the threats of environmental disaster—were wholly unforseen by Marx or his followers, as well as by conventional social observers; and that Marxists are as unable as anyone else to explain or project the forces of nationalism that will have to cope with these seismic disturbances.

As I have already made clear, however, I feel far more affirmatively with regard to the Marxist analysis of what capitalism *is,* whatever its problems in explaining what capitalism will become. The socioanalysis of the system, starting with the lowly commodity that contains within itself the disguised elements of the class struggle, strikes me as one of the most remarkable and illuminating acts of intellectual penetration of which we have record, truly meriting the comparison I have so often drawn with Plato and Freud. That penetrative capability is the unique, and, I think, the most remarkable and enduring, achievement of Marxism. It opens an understanding of society that is otherwise totally inaccessible, giving us the opportunity to grasp what we are, the necessary precondition to knowing what we might become.

FIVE

The Commitment to
Socialism

FROM MARX ONWARD, Marxism has always
been intended as more than a detached
program of research. It has been a union of theory and
praxis, an analysis of past and present undertaken to
serve as a guide to the attainment of a desired future.
That future is the establishment of socialism as a way-
station to an ultimate communism. The idea of socialism, and the struggle to attain it, are the life-giving
forces that sustain the work of Marxism.

Nonetheless, the relation of Marxism to socialism
has always been confused and troubled. Already in
Marx's time, the "unity" of theory and practice had led
to serious internal rifts as Marxist movements tried to
reconcile the objectives of Marx's teachings with the
confused ideas of the working classes, the zeal of anti-
communist police action, and the changing atmosphere
and institutional realities of capitalism. Thereafter
Marxism became more and more absorbed in internecine conflicts over the proper relation of theory and
practice, with polemics and tirades against the "ren-

egade Kautsky,'' the "social-democrat Bernstein,''
"Left-Wing infantilists,'' "deviationists,'' and the
like. And in the end, these theoretical disputes were
overshadowed by the terrible and tragic duel between
Stalin and Trotsky and their followers.

I shall not attempt to review that history of turmoil,
internal hatred, and general deterioration. For the death
of Stalin and the official revelation of his violence
precipitated a new issue to the fore. The crux of the
relation between Marxism and socialism ceased to be a
matter of correct strategy and tactics, but became instead the issue raised in the early pages of this book—
the responsibility that Marxism must bear for the actions
committed in its name.

Here it is not merely the furies of Stalinism that
define the issue. Beyond Stalinism remains the oppressive bureaucratic society of the Soviet Union, now so
far removed from the ideals of socialism held by most
Western Marxists that it has become fashionable (and
more than a little disingenuous) to relabel the Soviet
regime "state capitalism.'' Beyond the Soviet Union is
the disappointment of Cuba, or Yugoslavia, both repressive and authoritarian, if relatively benign, dictator-
ships by the admission of their own leaders. Beyond
Cuba lies China, under Mao Zedong one of the most
extraordinary examples of personal theocracy and mass
"thought control'' in history. And on the fringe lie the
atrocities and mockeries of "socialism''—all invoking
the name of Marx—that we find in Albania, Cambodia,
local African movements, and among terrorist groups.

To be sure, the matter is not open and shut. No one

would tolerate a judgment of Christianity that weighed in the balance only its complicity in torture, war, and exploitation. So, too, if Marxism is to be saddled with responsibility for Soviet or Chinese inhumanity, it must also be given credit for the immense material and cultural improvements that these regimes have brought to their peoples. This is not to say that a calculus of gain and loss will always tilt in favor of all Marxist regimes, but some such balancing effort must be made if our historical verdicts are not to be simply star-chamber proceedings.

With all such allowances, however, an immense moral problem remains. The specter of Communism that haunted capitalist Europe in 1848 has now come to haunt Marxism. For the totalitarianism and repressive policies that have accompanied the advent of "communism"—not once, but again and again—have raised the question of whether Marxism itself, consciously or unconsciously, by virtue of its method or its message, despite its protestations of democratic faith and socialist idealism, is not inextricably connected with the political catastrophes that "Marxist" socialism has brought.

Two arguments are advanced by those who believe this to be the case. The first is that the texture of Marxist thinking degenerates easily into dogma, that there is something inherently predisposed toward totalitarianism in the very cast of Marxist ideas.

It is certainly possible that some such intellectual "mind set" may characterize Marxist thought. But it is not the content of the ideas themselves that contains this danger, I believe. Instead, the danger lies in the feelings of a select discipleship generated among those who have accepted the ideas—a discipleship based on a penetration to hidden realities that is indeed offered by the dialectical, materialist, and socioanalytic perspectives opened to Marxism. This sense of having access to privileged insight leads all too easily to feelings of impatience or disdain for those who have failed to see the light; and worse than that, to an easy confusion of ignorance or disagreement with heresy or apostasy. Intolerant religiosity is not, of course, peculiar to Marxism, but the attitude may help explain the moral and intellectual arrogance that has marked the movement from early on.

A second argument ascribes the linkage between Marxism and repressive government to the systematic failure of Marxist theory to understand that political power exists as an ''independent'' force that must be buffered and contained by other institutions. Later we shall look more deeply into the substance of this charge, but at first account it is undeniably true that Marxism tends to relegate questions of political power to a secondary role, just as bourgeois thought tends to minimize or overlook the role of economic power. One of the consequences for Marxism is that the economic sphere is viewed only in its active, dynamic role. What is overlooked is that this selfsame sphere may also constitute a kind of state within a state, offering to its inhabitants some refuge from the exercise of political authority.

This is by no means to argue that a market system or a capitalist economy constitute infallible barriers against totalitarianism, as the rise of Nazi Germany and fascist Italy demonstrate. Yet, in less extreme cases, it seems plausible that the network of business enterprises and the economic rights of individuals—including, above all their right to withhold or offer their own labor as they wish—may constitute a barrier against, and a counterforce to, the unobstructed expansion of state power; and it is a damning fact that Marxist governments have not yet established—or even admitted the need for—such countervailing institutions of any kind.

It must be apparent, then, that I take seriously the charge that the propensity for an expansive and intolerant use of political power may exist within Marxist-oriented governments. Yet the extraordinary circumstances under which Marxist governments have come into the world make it impossible to draw a strict connection between any such propensity and the actualities of political life. Here three overriding circumstances should be borne in mind. The first is that Marxism is the main revolutionary force in the world today, and thereby becomes the natural gravitational center for movements of all kinds that seek to remedy poverty and to express outrage at the manipulation of humanity. Thus, cultlike alienated groups, terrorist organizations, liberation armies and the like rally to the banner of Marxism and use its vocabulary to express their demands and aspirations. As with Christianity in its most zealous days, and for much the same reasons, ''Marxism'' has become entangled in some of the worst as well as some of the best of human activity.

A second consideration is that a Marxist state, as any other, must establish its internal and external security. As a *revolutionary* regime, this entails problems of great difficulty. A Marxist government may well expect efforts to topple it from without—witness the cases of Cuba and Chile—and must anticipate strong resistance, perhaps even counterrevolution, from defeated groups within. Until its security is established, therefore, Marxist regimes will almost certainly have to resort to repressive measures for self-protection.

The third, well-known "defense" of Marxist political proclivities is that its revolutions have thus far occurred only in countries that have no liberal traditions, no long, hard-won experience with political tolerance, no prior commitment to democracy. Even in favored nations a Marxist revolution might have difficulty in maintaining political liberties—its failure to do so is all the more understandable in lands that have never known anything but authoritarian or despotic rule, and that have had no acquaintance whatsoever with civil or political liberties.

Thus, conventional arguments are not likely to resolve the problem of the relation of Marxist thought to practice one way or the other. If there are cogent reasons to expect Marxist regimes to display repressive tendencies in present-day circumstances, there are also plausible grounds for viewing these circumstances as exceptional and perhaps remediable. Beyond that, there is little to be said.

What is needed, then, is an approach to this critical

issue that will transcend the limitations of conventional argument. Is there such an approach? I think there is, if we are willing to consider the matter from another point of view. We must inquire into the idea of socialism as a new socioeconomic formation, a different mode of production, a possible next chapter of history as seen from a materialist perspective. Such an inquiry is, of course, an effort to apply a Marxist analysis to the objective for which Marxism exists—socialism itself. This will not definitively resolve the problems of freedom or political power within socialism—who could do that?—but it will force us to consider the question from another, and I think more useful, perspective.

(2)

Let us begin this difficult inquiry by reverting to the outline of humanity's historic journey that we sketched in Chapter III, a journey that began in the vague socioeconomic formation of "primitive communism" and that has proceeded slowly and irregularly into the pregnant period we call capitalism. Is there an overarching theme, a grand pattern, that can be discerned in this long, tortuous, often dead-ended journey? I think there are two such themes, although I must make clear that Marx himself never addressed the problem directly.

The first theme of world history is the gradual, cumulative, improvement of the forces of production—the technical means by which mankind provides for its continuance. Indeed, one reason why capitalism is so important in Marx's view of history is precisely because it is within this stage that the economic problem becomes "solved." As a consequence of the enormous emphasis that capitalism places on production, it is within capitalism that mankind finally overcomes the cramping constraints posed by a harsh and illiberal Nature. We can also see a second theme slowly unfolding, manifested in the gradual clarification of the social relationships of mankind. One by one, the enslaving ideas of the sacred authority of priests, the divine rights of kings, the inborn superiority of nobility, are unmasked, until at last there remains only the intricately defended rights of property, the most mystifying of all mankind's social relations. Here, too, capitalism is the staging area for the fullest development of that mystification and then for its ultimate dissolution.

The cogency of this majestic scheme of history is not a matter for our consideration now. Rather, we return to it because it poses an initial, elemental definition of socialism as a new socioeconomic formation. Socialism, for Marxism, becomes that phase of history in which mankind will be released both from the bondage of material insufficiency and from its servitude to the power of mystification. The release is not absolute. A Kingdom of Necessity, in Marx's words, remains: mankind must conduct its affairs within the bounds imposed by nature.[1] But the boundaries will have so

---

[1] "In fact [Marx writes], the realm of freedom actually begins only where labour which is determined by necessity and mundane considerations ceases; thus in the very nature of things it lies beyond the sphere of actual material production. Just as the savage must wrestle with Nature to satisfy his wants, to maintain and reproduce life, so must civilized man, and he must do so in all social formations and under all possible modes of production. With his development, this realm of

expanded that a new phase of historical development can begin—the first period of truly *human* history, wrote Engels.

As to the technologies, institutions, or cultures of that new phase Marx or Engels have nothing to say. But there is no mistaking their belief that the new social formation would make possible two profound changes in the nature of existence. The first of these is the transformation of labor, the activity that to Marx and his followers is the most profoundly "species-specific" of all human behavior. As Marx writes in a famous passage of *Capital*:

> We presuppose labour in a form that stamps it as exclusively human. A spider conducts operations that resemble those of a weaver and a bee puts to shame many an architect in the construction of its cells. But what distinguishes the worst of architects from the best of bees is this, that the architect raises his structure in imagination before he erects it in reality.[2]

In this kind of labor—thought realized in action—Marx finds the quintessential human activity,

---

physical necessity expands as a result of his wants; but, at the same time, the forces of production which satisfy these wants also increase. Freedom in this field can only consist in socialized man, the associated producers, rationally regulating their interchange with Nature, bringing it under their common control, instead of being ruled by it as the blind forces of Nature; and achieving this with the least expenditure of energy and under conditions most favorable to, and worthy of, their human nature. But it nonetheless still remains a realm of necessity. Beyond it begins that development of human energy which is an end in itself, the true realm of freedom, which, however, can blossom forth only with this realm of necessity as its basis. . . ." (*Capital*, III, p. 820). Marx does not mention any *psychological* Kingdom of Necessity that might place constraints on the social relations into which mankind is capable of entering, comparable to those that limit its relations of production. As we shall see, the failure of Marxism to fill in this lacuna, and to provide a theory of the personality as an underpinning for its view on politics, constitutes one of the most serious weaknesses in its relationship to socialism.

[2]*Capital*, I, p. 178.

an activity systematically deformed and denied under capitalist conditions of production. Thus a first objective for socialism is the restoration to man of the stolen powers of self-expression and fulfillment that lie in work. More than self-expression, work must become a means by which individuals may express and recognize their existence as social creatures. Describing such a society, in which producers are "human beings," Marx writes, perhaps rhapsodically:

In my production I would have objectified my individuality in its uniqueness . . . in your enjoyment or use of my product, I would have had the direct satisfaction of the awareness of having satisfied a human need through my work; . . . I would have had the satisfaction of having acted as an intermediary between you and the human species. . . . Our products would be so many mirrors from which our being would shine out to us. . . .[3]

We shall turn in due course to the problems posed by this central objective of socialism. But there remains the second strand of thought to be explored in the general vision of the "truly human history" of which socialism was to be the first phase. This is the idea of the emancipation of man from his eternal enthrallments, his realization of freedom.

Freedom is a complex idea in Marx, never fully explicated. But it is clear that Marx did not consider freedom to be exemplified by its manifestations in bourgeois society. Indeed, just as his animus against capitalism rests in part on its deformation of the human experience of work, so Marx inveighs against

[3]Quoted in Fetscher, *Marx and Marxism*, pp. 36–37.

capitalism for its deformation of the idea of freedom. In *The German Ideology,* Marx and Engels write:

In imagination individuals seem freer under the dominance of the bourgeoisie than before, because their conditions of life seem accidental; in reality, of course, they are less free, because they are more subjected to the violence of things.[4]

Plainly the concept of freedom uppermost in Marx's mind is freedom from economic forces and their "fetishization"—in particular freedom from the pressure of the social conditions that drive men into the exploitative and mystifying wage-labor relationship.

Thus Marx stresses that freedom in bourgeois society is only a particular kind of freedom, not freedom "in general." The freedom of bourgeois civilization rests on the rights of men and women to enter into contracts and to dispose as they wish of their personal property, above all their labor power. Needless to say, this sheltering cloak protects the millionaire as well as the working person. But bourgeois freedom also represents a *diminution* of freedom of a kind for which capitalist society has no use. This is the freedom from social abandonment, freedom from the perils of abrupt dismissal. With regard to these freedoms, feudal times were the superior of capitalism, at least in capitalism's early phases. Of course this freedom from insecurity under feudalism was realized as inadequately and unfairly as the freedom of contract under capitalism. But there is no denying that such a right existed in theory, as do the

[4]Karl Marx and Friedrich Engels, *The German Ideology* (New York: International Publishers, 1947, 1966), p. 77. See also *Grundrisse* pp. 156–159, 161–165.

rights of property for all under capitalism. Thus Marx sees the transition into capitalism as a mixture of gain and loss: individuals are freed from the fetters of feudal life only to be constrained by the economic imperatives of capitalism.

Freedom under socialism would therefore entail the release of individuals from these imperatives. This in turn requires that the blind and impersonal forces of economic life be replaced by a conscious direction of the interaction of men and women with nature and among themselves. The "laws" of capitalist motion, including the laws of exchange and competition, must give way to the conscious regulation and coordination of work. Where blind economic obedience was, conscious political will must be.

(3)

The reestablishment of the importance of truly human work, and the transcendence of the barriers of bourgeois freedom, thereby become implicit aims of socialism in Marx's view. As we have noted, Marx himself carefully refrained from "utopian" efforts to translate those aims into institutional form. Here and there a few passages, some touched with a millennial flavor, others more matter of fact, give us glimpses of socialism as he imagined it. In *The German Ideology*, for example, we read about socialism as a society in which one would be free ". . . to hunt in the morning, fish in the afternoon, rear cattle in the evening, criticize after dinner, just as I have a mind, without ever becoming hunter, fisherman, shepherd, or critic." Again, in glancing at passages in *Capital* we find references to "associations of working-men" who freely regulate their own labor and determine the terms of their intercourse with nature.[5]

Beyond these flashes, not a word is to be found with regard to the organizational structure that will make possible this restoration of the wholeness of work, or of the degree of technical complexity of production compatible with it. All such questions Marx relegated to the future.[6]

Not until Lenin do we encounter an attempt to sketch an idealized framework for the organization of socialism—an attempt that also leaves more unsaid than said. In *State and Revolution* Lenin writes:

Accounting and control—these are the *chief* things necessary for the organizing and correct functioning of the *first phase* of Communist society. *All* citizens are here transformed into hired employees of the State, which is made up of the armed workers. *All* citizens become employees and workers of *one* national State "syndicate." All that is required is that they should work equally, should regularly do their share of work,

[5]Marx and Engels, *Germany Ideology*, p. 22; *Capital*, I, pp. 171–72, 173; IV, *Theories of Surplus Value* (Moscow, Progress Publishers, 1963, 1969), p. 820; *Grundrisse*, pp. 705–6, 712.

[6]It is worth remarking that Marx also had little to say about the distribution of income appropriate to socialism. However, in *The Gotha Program* (1875), he ridiculed the notion that socialism required the equalization of income payments, and wrote the famous passage below that indicated the long-term nature of the transformation that he expected:

In a higher phase of communist society, after the enslaving subordination of individuals under division of labour, and therewith also the antithesis between mental and physical labour, has vanished; after labour, from a mere means of life, has itself become the prime necessity of life; after the productive forces have also increased with the all-round development of the individual, and all the springs of cooperative wealth flow more freely—only then can the narrow horizon of bourgeois rights be fully left behind and society inscribe on its banners: from each according to his ability, to each according to his needs! (Marx, *Critique of the Gotha Program*, from Tucker, *Marx-Engels Reader*, p. 531.)

and should receive equal pay. The accounting and control necessary for this have been *simplified* by capitalism to the utmost, 'til they have become the extraordinarily simple operations of watching, recording and issuing receipts, within the reach of anybody who can read and write and knows the first four rules of arithmetic.[7]

Extended comment is unnecessary. The statement reflects an extraordinary, although in Lenin's day widespread, faith in the "rationalization" of production that had presumably already taken place under capitalism, making possible its transfer to socialist management with a minimum of disruption. It is Veblen's image of the technocratic society where production is "run" by engineers no longer encumbered with a "price system"; a society conceived (in Lenin's words) as "one office and one factory" under the direction of an administrative state guarded by the "armed workers." Lenin's vision is a fantasy that resembles the stylized images of cities of the future popular with architects such as le Corbusier or the designer-engineers who created the famous General Motors Futurama in the World's Fair of 1937.

The history of the Marxist depiction of socialism since that time can be described as an awkward retreat from Lenin's vision to an uneasy confrontation with the technological and organizational demands imposed by the industrial apparatus inherited from the capitalist past, or created by socialist regimes as part of their general subscription to an industrialized method of pro-

---

[7]Lenin's italics. *A Handbook of Marxism*, ed. E. Burns (New York: Random House, 1935), pp. 757–8.

duction. The monotonous, often dangerous and dirty, high-speed processes of mining, manufacture, and transportation—not to mention the tedium of administration—differ little from capitalist to socialist nations, allowance being made for the level of general development from which each nation begins. Out of consideration of national defense, efforts to build a satisfactory social support structure, or simply because of their acceptance of the goal of "growth," socialist nations have sought to make their peace with modern technology. This has necessitated, on the one hand, the development of intricate bureaucracies and planning systems; on the other, the virtual abandonment of Marx's vision of labor raised to the level of work. At best the socialist goal of the humanization of labor has found expression in the encouragement of workers' participation in the design and pace of their tasks (always with the goal of "efficiency" in mind), and in an assumption of limited managerial responsibilities. Although in very different ways, these goals have been particularly stressed in Mao's China and in Yugoslavia, to what lasting effect we cannot yet say.

How far this humanization of work may proceed in the distant future is a matter before which modern Marxism has made no significant pronouncements. Perhaps none can be made, when so much depends on the rivalries of international life, on the depletion of resources, on the willingness or ability of socialist governments to intervene in the formation of material standards of life. Imaginably, Marx's Kingdom of Necessity could lighten the necessary obedience of its subjects through the sharing of work, the rotation of tasks, the redesign of equipment, the willing surrender of "efficiency" for self-fulfillment. Imaginably, too, the Kingdom of Necessity could become a labor camp. The continuing hope of socialism rests with Marx's conviction that mankind's inescapable labor can become the means of its self-expression, not of its self-imprisonment. Whether or not history will justify this central faith of Marxism is a matter that we will not know for a long time.

Whatever the long-term possibilities with regard to the restructuring of work, short-term realities must be faced. Any society that aspires to create a new socio-economic basis will require the exercise of unprecedented authority over economic activity. The huge productive apparatus of contemporary industrial society will have to be adapted to a different set of outputs, if the quality of life under socialism is to be different from that under capitalism. The nature of the production process itself, now dominated by high-speed technology and an inhuman division of labor, will have to be redesigned, if the work experience of socialism is to differ from that of capitalism. And of course the distribution of income must undergo radical change unless, once again, the economic class structure of the old society is not to reappear, perhaps with new occupants, in the new.

All this requires the use of political command. Indeed, the creation of socialism as a new mode of production can properly be compared to the moral equivalent of war—war against the old order, in this case—

156

and will need to amass and apply the power commensurate with the requirements of a massive war. This need not entail the exercise of command in an arbitrary or dictatorial fashion, but certainly it requires the curtailment of the central economic freedom of bourgeois society, namely the right of individuals to own, and therefore to withhold if they wish, the means of production, including their own labor. The full preservation of this bourgeois freedom would place the attainment of socialism at the mercy of property owners who could threaten to deny their services to society—and again I refer to their labor, not just to material resources—if their terms were not met.

Can some preserve of economic rights be maintained under the conditions of a radical socialist transformation? We do not know. But it is customary to start from the assumption that curtailing property rights, especially the right to dispose of our labor as we please, implies a serious diminution of economic freedom. I do not wish to shrug off the clear possibility of violating human dignity under the injunction of "building socialism." Nevertheless, if we are to take seriously the premise that socialism as a new socioeconomic formation requires the radical reconstruction of the mode of production, we must be willing to face the question from a different point of view. We must then ask whether rights and freedoms will not have to be redrawn in such a way as to facilitate, not block, this overriding objective. From such a perspective our attitude necessarily changes. Freedom does not necessarily diminish as a whole, even if we curtail or surrender property

157

rights in labor, provided we esteem more highly the freedoms gained from a redesigned quality of worklife and from the abolition of the "accidental" pressures of the marketplace.

I do not raise this possibility to argue the case, but to force us to confront the issue of work and freedom from the only vantage point that will shed some light on the relation of Marxist thought and Marxist practice. For the problem then becomes that of acceding before, or finding ways to surmount, the exigencies of the historical transformation that must be achieved *if socialism is to be a new socioeconomic formation, and not merely an improvement of relations that are essentially capitalist in nature.*

I stress this last thought, because it is of the essence. We have seen that the experience of work, for Marx, and by extension for Marxism, is a central defining element of socialism. To create the conditions of work envisaged by Marx, in which individuals are released from the cramping and confining subservience to "detail labor," will require a radical redesign of the material base of society. For that transformation to take place, the most thoroughgoing alteration will be required in the technology and the social structure of society. And for such an alteration, an enormous exercise of authority will be called for.

To be sure, once the transformation has been made and the new technical and social arrangement set into place, the direction of the system may require only a minimum of direct command, being entrusted to the inertia of tradition, or to public consensus arrived at by democratic means. A greater sense of economic liberty and a higher level of working morale may prevail in such a society than exists under capitalism. But it would be foolhardy—and worse, deceptive—to expect that the transition itself could be made without recourse to massed command, or to deny that the transition will pose grave dangers for the abuse of that command or for its emplacement on a long-lasting basis.

(4)

These considerations return us to the matter of freedom in a larger sense. Marx, we recall, was interested in analyzing the *unfreedom* hidden within the bourgeois conception of freedom, a conception that was founded on its celebration of economic liberty.

Not surprisingly, the first formulation of the freedoms to be sought under socialism concentrated almost entirely on the abolition of class-bound economic unfreedoms. Of the ten points of the *Manifesto,* five are exclusively aimed at undoing the property basis for such unfreedom: abolition of property in land; graduated income taxes; abolition of inheritance; confiscation of emigree property; centralization of credit in state hands. Three underpin a new freedom from want by socializing production: nationalization of communication and transportation; enlargement of a state production sector and of state planning; and the establishment of "industrial armies." Only the last two points—the "gradual abolition of the distinction between town and country" (by a more equitable distribution of the population), and "free education for all children," together with the combination of education and labor—are essentially *social* in their intent, although of course vast social consequences would flow from the application of the previous eight economic objectives.

What strikes our sensitized twentieth-century eyes is the absence of any reference to those aspects of social and political life in which we today see the greatest dangers to freedom. The *Manifesto* has no aspirations or declarations with regard to political dissent, civil rights, social or sexual emancipation, or—above all— intellectual freedom.[8] The main battlegrounds on which liberty has been defeated in socialist countries are thus not even identified as strategic territory by Marx and Engels.

Before we explore this one-sided conception of freedom, we must recognize the rationale for Marx's economic emphasis. This was his desire to reveal that the bourgeois definition of "freedom," with its foundation in property, presupposed a conception of man as an isolated atom of society. Marx's conception of man, as we have seen, was "the ensemble of social relations." The conventional bourgeois celebrations of political, social, perhaps even intellectual freedoms interested Marx little because discussion of these aspects of freedom proceeded from a base that he found faulty; namely, an idea of "mankind" as a mere collection of isolated individuals, a society of hermits, each wholly

---

[8]The *Manifesto* does consider the accusation against communism that it would abolish the family, using this as a springboard from which to launch an attack on bourgeois notions of the family. But the *Manifesto* contains no specific reforms or general revolutionary goals for family relations.

divorced from his or her fellow individuals save for a network of contractual arrangements by which the (economic) interactions of society were regulated and assured. Of an original, ever-present, never-to-be-extirpated *sociality* of mankind, bourgeois thought knew nothing. Even when it spoke of man as a "social" creature, the idea of man that it held in mind was that of an autonomous, insular individual.[9]

Thus for Marx the problem of freedom lay initially in revealing the peculiar and untenable conceptions of "the individual" in bourgeois thought. The problem of liberty that engrossed John Stuart Mill—the problem of the maximum permissible intervention of society into the presumably autonomous life of individuals—was never seriously examined by Marx because he was more interested in a critique of its starting point—namely, that individuals were in some sense prior to, and imaginable without, society.

This most emphatically does not mean that Marx was not interested in *individuation*, the development of the differing capabilities of human beings. He even went so far as to define communism as that society in which "subjective *human* sensibility" could be de-

[9]See *Grundrisse*, p. 84: "The human being is in the most literal sense *zoon politikon*, not merely a gregarious animal, but an animal which can individuate itself only in the midst of society." With extraordinary insight, Marx points out that the very elements singled out by Adam Smith as celebrating the sociality of man in fact celebrate his unsociality. Marx writes: "*Division of labor* and *exchange* are the two *phenomena* in connection with which the political economist boasts of the social character of his science and in the same breath gives expression to the contradiction in his science—the establishment of society through unsocial, particular interests." From Lucio Colletti, *From Rousseau to Lenin* (New York and London: Monthly Review Press, 1972), p. 158. I owe the phrase "a society of hermits" to Martha Stires.

161

veloped to its greatest extent.[10] The question he left unexplored, however, is the tension between the individuation of character and behavior, and the unity and conformity necessary for social cohesion. This is a tension whose difficulties are certain to be increased in a socialist or communist society that has left behind the "cash nexus" that both encourages and restrains so much "individualistic" behavior under capitalism. The crucial question is then posed as to the extent to which individuation along deviant social or political lines would be possible without rupturing the bonds of sociality itself. This is a matter whose implications we will investigate later.

First, however, we must note another attribute of Marx's social conception of "the individual"; namely, the difficulties raised by such a view with regard to the roots of political power.

The individual to Marx is "the ensemble of social relations," to repeat the luminous phrase once more. However indispensable as an antidote to the bourgeois conception, the depiction of man as a creation of society presents as many problems as the conception of man as a primordial individual. For if the human animal is wholly created by society—not by an innate "nature"—it is impossible to define any limits to its behavior, save those given by physiology. Such a

---

[10]From James Miller, *History and Social Existence* (Berkeley: University of California Press, 1979), p. 26. Miller's book is a very interesting discussion of Marx's concern with the issue of individuation, although it does not raise the question above.

"plastic" notion of humanity—the idea that mankind makes itself—is generally regarded by Marxists as a great source of inspiration. And of course that is true, compared with the view that humanity is consigned forever to some miserable state, whether by Providence, nature, or human nature.

Nevertheless, there is a severe price to be paid for a view of the human being as without any definition other than that created by its social setting. For the individual thereupon becomes the expression of social relations binding him or her together with other individuals who are likewise nothing but the creatures of *their* social existences. We then have a web of social determinations that has no points of anchorage other than in our animal bodies. The expressions of love and hate, sympathy and distaste, admiration and envy, that play such powerful roles in society, have no primal sources, no wellsprings. In effect, the conception of the individual as solely the ensemble of its social relations denies the presence of the human psyche as an irreducible element of reality, an element as solid as flesh and blood.

With such a denial we are deprived of understanding or anticipating much social behavior. This is the case above all in the crucial area of political behavior, where Marxist theoretical shortcomings have been most striking and where its political actions most reprehensible. We have already noted that Marxism in general has failed to foresee—or after the event to explain—the drive to enlarge the scope of political power; a drive that seems as boundless in scale as that which Marxism expects of the drive for economic power. Instead, Marxism has been constantly taken by surprise by political tendencies that are part of the common wisdom of not only bourgeois, but ancient and Asiatic and aristocratic conceptions of politics. To most Marxists, the wariness regarding the political appetites of man expressed by Plato or Aristotle, Machievelli or Hobbes, J. S. Mill or Tocqueville only reveals the culture and class bound-edness of the authors, who fail to perceive the curative possibilities of a changed social environment. What is overlooked is the possibility that within these admitted-ly culture- and class-bound remarks there may yet reside an element of truth, namely, that humans contain "domineering" and "acquiescing" elements in their natures even in the most benign settings—elements that prudent individuals will recognize, and whose presence they will ignore, only at their own peril. The conse-quence, as the history of this century makes all too plain, is that politics becomes the Achilles' heel of socialism, just as economics is that of capitalism—an Achilles' heel not just as an area in which dysfunctions tend to be concentrated, but also as the area in which the capacity for self-understanding is most inherently limited.[11]

[11]Is there a possibility that Marxism could remedy this lack by embracing a Freudian theory of the personality? Much interest has been aroused by this prospect in recent years, and some rapprochement between Marxism and psychoanalysis has been attempted, above all in the Frankfurt School and its successors. My opinion however, is that an unbridgeable chasm finally divides the two, despite many similarities and complementarities. The problem lies in the necessity for psychoanalysis to assume certain "givens" within the structure of the human psyche if its theory of the personality is not to be merely a foundationless regress to "society." This means, at the very least, that the personality, as the partial product of these givens, cannot be altered as rapidly or thoroughly as would be the case were it solely the product of social conditioning. In turn, this admission drastically limits the Marxist expectations for social change, because it must recognize the persis-

Only as part of the aftermath of Stalinism, has the exclusive focus on economic freedom begun to give way to a recognition, still marked by uncertainty, that a political "sphere" may exist independent of the economic. In addition, the issues of feminism and racism have emerged as problems for Marxism that cannot be adequately dealt with by the categories of class relationship on which Marxist explanations of power and domination are solely based.

Still today, however, Marxist thought is almost entirely indifferent to, or ignorant of, any systematic consideration of the means of containing political power. The idea of creating a semi-independent structure of rights—comparable to, although perhaps not including, property rights (conventionally defined)—as a potential counterforce to the state, remains completely unexplored. Nor has there been any interest in examining such questions as the appropriate distribution of functions and powers among the organs of government, the election or removal of judges or civil servants, the appropriate behavior of elected representatives, and similar problems of democratic life. It is equally silent with respect to such problems as the means of assuring an independent press, the means by which political dissenters can be assured of income, the methods by which party elites can be controlled, etc. The most dangerous tendencies of political life are thus almost totally neglected in Marxist thought, or declared to be

---

tence of latent human traits, however dramatic may be the alteration in manifest activity. See R.L. Heilbroner, "Marxism, Psychoanalysis, and the Problem of a Unified Theory of Behavior," *Social Research* (Autumn 1975), pp. 414–432.

resolvable by "participatory democracy," a mode of political behavior that is never institutionally described.

(5)

These reflections are familiar enough to anyone who has considered the problem of power in its relation to socialism. Yet, as with the question of the command function during the arduous period of transition, it may be that we tend to approach the matter from the wrong side. That is, we take for granted the nature and specifications of the political and social and intellectual rights and freedoms to be expected under the new social formation of socialism; but we do not inquire into the compatibility of these rights and freedoms, as we know them in a bourgeois setting, with the requirements of the new order.

The crucial element here is easily identified. Underlying the bourgeois culture of capitalism, as we have seen, is the all-important idea of the primacy of the individual. This conception of man, we recall, was the occasion for some of Marx's most biting criticisms of capitalism. His view, and the view of all Marxists since his time, stressed the idea of the individual *as a product of society*. One would therefore expect that a socialist order would attempt to realize this conception in its values, precepts, and social indoctrination as pervasively and insistently as capitalist society proclaims the central importance of the individual.

Indeed, it is difficult to conceive socialism as a new socioeconomic formation without such an all-embracing emphasis; just as it is difficult to imagine it

166

without a pervasive reconstitution of the methods of production or distribution. The main emphasis of a socialist culture must be on the enhancement of the social consciousness of its citizens, not only as an awareness of each person's obligations toward the collectivity of others, but even more, as an awareness of the moral priority of society over the rights of its individual members.

This socialized viewpoint, which we must expect to be inculcated with all the educational and propaganda instruments of socialism, implies a lower estimation of individuation than we find in bourgeois society. The very idea of individual "difference" becomes a challenge to the primacy of the collectivity, rather than a self-evident consequence of the primacy of the individual. This lessened estimation of individuation is not, of course, new. Primitive, classical, or medieval society did not believe that a healthy society was one that encouraged variations on a given theme, much less variations in the given theme. Quite the opposite, the ideal of a healthy society was conceived as a core of social, political, and religious beliefs that society had agreed upon; and departures from, much less rejections of, those beliefs were regarded with suspicion as sources of the gravest moral as well as practical consequences.

I suspect that a socialist society, striving to overcome the alienation and fragmentation of bourgeois life through the cultivation of a pervasive social consciousness, must also regard its culture in this fashion. The ethos of a socialist socio-economic formation is therefore likely to be "sacred" rather than "profane," morally accountable rather than amorally expedient, fraught with spiritual significance rather than merely with pragmatic options. The calculus of utilitarianism is apt to give way to the calculus of personal responsibility. A socialist society, to be sharply differentiated from a capitalist one, should be as suffused and preoccupied with the idea of a collective moral purpose as is bourgeois society with the idea of individual personal achievement.

The ideological image of socialism, as a new socioeconomic formation, seems likely therefore to resemble that of a religious society. As such it may support or even encourage certain forms of what we would call individualism. It may inspire saints; it may lead to extreme feats of courage, asceticism, or self-sacrifice; it may result in wide varieties of psychic experience. What seems unlikely is that it will spontaneously generate, or easily tolerate, sociopolitical ideas or behavior that challenge or threaten the cohering vision of the society itself. For the toleration of diverse sociopolitical ideas characteristic of the most advanced bourgeois culture attests not only to the libertarian ideals of these societies; it testifies as well to a lack of any deep religious or moral significance attaching to most ideas. The "marketplace of ideas," the common phrase used to celebrate bourgeois intellectual freedom, unwittingly reveals the secular, commoditylike view that attaches to much bourgeois thought, where even the most radical views are rapidly absorbed as chic, or even turned to profitable account as part of the commercialization of life. A primitive, a priestly, a Catholic, or, I believe, a socialist society would not view ideas with such indifference.

In making this suggestion I do not wish to imply that a socialist society would of necessity be one of severe oppression or of totalitarian cast. Stalinism is a pathology of socialism, Hitlerism being the apposite example for capitalism. To the extent that a socialist socioeconomic formation attains its objective of nurturing citizens who share a common conception of socialist life, the need for oppression and restraint should diminish. A socialist society can as naturally produce socialist-minded citizens as a capitalist society produces capitalist-minded individuals. Nor need the citizens of a socialist world feel emotionally, intellectually, or politically deprived because they live in a culture that regards certain opinions as heretical and therefore forbids them. To the eyes of socialists in the future, the world of high bourgeois civilization with its relatively unsupervised intellectual or political or social life may well appear as the unhappy and undesirable consequence of the rootlessness and false consciousness of capitalist life, as little to be regretted as the Saturnalia of Rome or the self-indulgences of the courts of monarchical Europe.

Thus the freedoms associated with a socialism that is "beyond" capitalism will be of a different kind than our own. Indeed, how could that not be the case if socialism is to be a radically new setting for mankind? Why should we expect that it would wish to encourage the political, social, sexual, or intellectual diversity that we project unthinkingly as the desired goal of socialist life? If socialism is to be a socioeconomic formation that is qualitatively different from, and not the mere perfection of, bourgeois society, we must expect that its definition of social life must express decisive departures from bourgeois ideals. That is, it must be more than a realization of the best of bourgeois aspirations freed of their crippling economic understructure. We may, of course, hope that socialism will wash away all that is petty and narcissistic in the bourgeois celebration of individuality, while retaining that which is of solid intellectual and aesthetic worth. But this can only be a hope, not an expectation. As a new social order, socialism must discover its own conceptions of the proper relationship between each individual and society. And whereas some socialists may remain as staunchly ''libertarian'' as some bourgeois have remained pious, it seems to me as unlikely that a socialist civilization will be fundamentally interested in what we call liberty as that a bourgeois civilization will be fundamentally interested in what its predecessors called piety.

(6)

These considerations will distress or outrage many readers, for they make clear that the relation between Marxism and socialism is not what it is commonly thought to be. The practice of Marxism is not an effort to create a kind of ''socialism'' that embodies the highest ideals of contemporary, bourgeois society. It is, rather, the effort to bring into being a new social order, *differ-*

ent from and beyond bourgeois society, and therefore
embodying institutions or ideals that may not be attractive, or even acceptable, to those of us who are situated
in, and profoundly influenced by, bourgeois thought.
Such reflections stretch, perhaps to the breaking point,
the tensions of being for *and* against Marxism, not for *or*
against it. Indeed, they make us uncertain as to what
"for" and "against" mean, when they refer to a new
social system, a new period of history, another chapter
of human existence.

It is, of course, possible to side-step this agonizing
issue by redefining socialism, and designating it not as a
new socioeconomic formation, but only as a movement
that presses against the institutions of capitalism, seeking the general social goal of "equality." This is, in
fact, the nature of the movements that are called
socialist, or social-democratic, in many advanced
nations—movements that are certainly of the greatest
importance for human well-being. They may, indeed,
be the very best that can be done, if one sums up the
prospects of socialism as a new social formation, and
decides *against,* not *for.*

The difficulty is that these movements of reform
are, by their nature, unable to attempt a radical change
in the material base of society, because the effort to do
so would bring them directly into the dangerous areas
we have discussed. They must therefore attempt to
realize their goals within the socioeconomic confines of
capitalism, because it is within these confines that the
liberties and freedoms dear to them are protected, however imperfectly. The effort of such reform movements

is therefore to create a socialistic capitalism, or a bourgeois socialism, more or less in the image of Sweden.

The question is how far such reformist movements can go without bringing down the underlying capitalist order, with unforeseeable consequences; or at what point it becomes necessary to hold back further reform because the underlying order is in danger of perishing. Whether an advanced socialistic capitalism would be a stable, or a satisfying, social system—the last, highest phase of capitalist society—is a matter that we cannot predict, but that we may discover, if present trends continue, within our own lifetime.

What remains open to question is whether Marxism itself will survive in a socialism of a truly revolutionary kind. The answer, it seems to me, hinges on whether Marxism is ultimately to be an ideology or a critical philosophy. As an ideology, its usefulness will be spent with the attainment of its objective. It may perhaps become fixed as the official credo of the new order, proclaiming in a dialectical vocabulary the emancipation of humankind from the capitalist epoch and the fulfillment of the species—animal man, in the state of socialism to which Marxism has led it. Marxism would in that case survive only to become a new fetter on human development, a fetter proclaiming that the achievement of socialism was the completion of the historic task of man; or perhaps it will retain a promised future attainment of pure communism as a vent for mankind's unsatisfied yearnings.

Because Marxism bears so many resemblances to a

universal Church in endowing human existence with meaning and purpose, it is entirely possible that its philosophy will end, as has that of so many universal churches, in mere ideology and theology. But Marxism contains—or better, marxisms contain—the possibility for more than that. A dialectical view of reality, enlarging our view of things with a tension and contradictoriness that is lacking in other philosophic perspectives, should help clarify our knowledge of the world. A materialist view of history will enrich our understanding of the past and of the present, as long as the processes of production play a powerful role in human affairs and exert such enormous influences over the stratification of society. The mysteries and movements of capitalism will interest scholars, and will need to be explained to ordinary citizens, for decades or generations to come, until capitalism is as distant a memory as feudalism is to ourselves. And socialism—the Grail of Marxism—must continue to exert its influence as long as humanity suffers the unnecessary bondages imposed by its own social organization, a condition that is certain to persist for generations.

The test of Marxism thus emerges in its relation to socialism, not to capitalism. Accordingly, it will be a long time before that test has determined whether Marxism is eventually to be relegated to the museum of antiquated or fossilized ideas, or whether it can continue as one of the ever-renewed endowments that mankind has created for itself. Alas, we will all be dead before that determination is made. But from Marx himself we can fashion a motto that may serve Marxism well. ''The philosophers have heretofore interpreted the world," said Marx in his ninth "thesis" on Feuerbach; "The thing, however, is to change it." In our times and henceforth, change is upon the world, in large part inspired and guided by Marxism itself. The task now is to understand it.

Index

accumulation of capital, 38, 50,
117–19
agriculture, 100–101, 122
alienation, 70–74, 167
class struggle and, 72–74,
85–86
*Alienation, Marx's Conception of
Man in Capitalist Society*
(Ollman), 57*n*, 73*n*
Althusser, Louis, 17*n*, 83*n*
ambiguity, 57, 58
anarchy, 123, 132–34, 137
Anderson, Perry, 62*n*, 88*n*
Anti-Dühring (Engels), 63–64, 74,
135
antithesis, 42
Aristotle, 96–97, 104*n*, 164
artisans, 100–101, 125
Asiatic mode of production, 64,
119

bargaining power, 108, 109–10,
112–13, 114
Becoming, 33, 35, 36
Being, 33, 35, 36
Bell, Daniel, 19*n*
Bernstein, Richard, 31*n*
Blackwell, Ronald, 93*n*–94*n*
bourgeois freedom, 145, 150–52,
157–58, 159, 160–61,
168–69
Braverman, Harry, 117*n*

Bukharin, Nikolai, 93*n*
Burnshaw, Stanley, 55*n*
business enterprises, 40, 50–51,
118, 145
centralization of capital in, 129
as corporations, 112, 133

capital, 37, 45, 72, 116–19
accumulation of, 38, 50,
117–19
concentration and
centralization of, 124–26,
129
deceptive appearance of, 17
domination through, 117
internationalization of, 129,
132–34
as "self-expanding value," 116,
133–34
wealth and, 103–5
Capital (Marx), 34*n*, 52*n*, 62*n*,
93*n*, 116*n*, 149, 153
on commodities, 95, 97, 101
relevance of, 17–18, 19
subtitle of, 17
"The Working Day" in, 108
capitalism, 19, 24, 40, 74
alienation in, 72, 167
class struggle in, 69–70, 73,
114, 117–18
contradictions and, 38–39, 50,
121–26, 133

Index

Index

Lowe, A., 128*n*
Lukács, Georg, 75*n*, 120*n*, 134
Lull, Raymond de, 104*n*
Luxemburg, Rosa, 93*n*,120*n*,133

Mably, Abbé, 119
Machiavelli, Niccolò, 164
machinery, 116, 121
  surplus value and, 110,
    121–22, 123
Making of Marx's Capital, The
  (Rosdolsky), 52*n*
Mandel, Ernest, 46*n*, 57*n*, 114*n*
Mantoux, Paul, 101*n*
Mao Zedong, 142, 155
markets, 111, 114, 118, 132, 158
  international, 93*n*, 133
  for labor, 100–101
Marx, Karl, 69, 81, 125, 153*n*,
    173–74
  on breakdown of capitalism,
    125–26
  on capital, 116, 118
  on class struggle, 73*n*
  on communism, 70, 71, 161–62
  conflicting interpretations of,
    19
  on "dictatorship of the
    proletariat," 73
  focus of, 22, 93–94
  Hegel's influence on, 33–37
  on "individual," 46, 162, 166
  level of reality discovered by,
    16–17
  on materialist interpretation of
    history, 62
  persisting influence of, 15–18
  on science, 47–48
  two historical conceptions of,
    87*n*
  see also Capital; Grundrisse

"Marx: from One Vision of
  History to Another"
  (Lefort), 87*n*
Marx and Marxism (Fetscher), 34*n*,
  150*n*
Marxism:
  base and superstructure in,
    82–84, 134–35
  commitment to socialism in,
    21–22, 27, 31–32, 141–74
  defining of, 19–23
  expanded scope of, 22
  future in, 21–22, 23, 27, 31–32,
    86, 87, 137, 141–74
  identity and unity in, 20–23
  as ideology vs. critical
    philosophy, 172–73
  institutional realization of, *see*
    Marxist states
  millennial assumptions in, 87,
    152
  as "necessary" philosophy,
    24–25
  political power as viewed in,
    144–45, 160, 163–66
  problems in consideration of,
    19–26, 32–33, 41–43,
    51–52, 82–89
  psychoanalysis and, 19, 149*n*,
    164*n*–65*n*
  religion and, 19, 80, 84, 168,
    172–73
  as revolutionary doctrine,
    25–26, 63–64, 125, 127,
    134–35, 145–46
  social science and, 47–51
  socioanalysis of capitalism in,
    17–18, 21, 39, 61, 69–70,
    93–138
  synthesis and, 22–23, 42
  uniqueness of, 81

182

Index

Index

335.4 Heilbroner, Robert
HEI   L.

    Marxism, for and
    against

AUG 19 1980	DATE		
AUG 30 1980	MAR 20 1985		
SEP 19 1980	APR 12 1985		
NOV 22 1980	NOV 27 1985		
DEC 20 1980			
JUN 27 1981			
JUL 14 1981			
SEP 12 1981			
APR 3 1982			
SEP 2 1983			
JAN 31 1985			